THE MAKING
OF ARAB NEWS

THE MAKING
OF ARAB NEWS

Noha Mellor

ROWMAN & LITTLEFIELD PUBLISHERS, INC.
Lanham • *Boulder* • *New York* • *Toronto* • *Oxford*

ROWMAN & LITTLEFIELD PUBLISHERS, INC.

Published in the United States of America
by Rowman & Littlefield Publishers, Inc.
A wholly owned subsidary of The Rowman & Littlefield Publishing Group, Inc.
4501 Forbes Boulevard, Suite 200, Lanham, MD 20706
www.rowmanlittlefield.com

P.O. Box 317, Oxford OX2 9RU, UK

British Library Cataloguing in Publication Information Available

Library of Congress Cataloging-in-Publication Data
Mellor, Noha, 1969-
 The making of Arab news / Noha Mellor.
   p. cm.
 Includes bibliographical references and index.
 ISBN 0-7425-3818-4 (cloth : alk. paper) — ISBN 0-7425-3819-2 (pbk. : alk. paper)
 1. Press—Arab countries. 2. Journalism—Arab countries. I. Title.
PN4731.M398 2005
070.4'0917'67—dc22

                              2004017292

Printed in the United States of America

♾™ The paper used in this publication meets the minimum requirements of American
National Standard for Information Sciences—Permanence of Paper for Printed Library
Materials, ANSI/NISO Z39.48-1992.

To my best friend, Rob Mellor

Contents

Tables and Figures

Tables

Figures

Preface

A S A NATIVE ARAB LIVING in Europe and working in the field of media—both as a scholar and a journalist—I have had the privilege of being able to access information and publications in both English and Arabic. I have deliberately chosen to share this privilege with my readers by consistently presenting the views of Arab scholars and professionals side by side with the views of their western, and particularly American, counterparts. In this book, I present *my* own views of the current developments on the Arab media scene. Some readers, Arab or other nationals, might not share these views or agree with my evaluation of these developments. Nonetheless, I hope this book sparks a debate on the future of the Arab news media from the point of view of scholars and journalists as well as the general public. I particularly welcome any comments on the content of this book, which can be delivered to my e-mail address: noha@mellor.com

I have both words of thanks and apology to present in this space. Firstly, I would like to thank Thomas Petruso for his invaluable editorial help. Moreover, I acknowledge my gratitude to the *International Herald Tribune* for allowing the reproduction of parts of its articles. I would also like to thank *Al Sharq Al Awsat*, *Al Hayat*, and *Al Rai Al am* for giving me permission to cite some of their articles. The portions of the articles cited in Arabic are accompanied by English translations, which are my own. I have deliberately made the translations as simple, and at times as literal, as they could be to show the effect in the source text.

Finally, a word of apology is in order: The great technological progress in the field of publishing has enabled scholars like me to access a vast amount of (recent) articles and publications online. However, these are in different formats with different page numbering than in the original printed text. The effect of this is that in a few places in the book, I have not been able to give the precise page number as in the original cited article since I depended on the online subscription versions of the publication.

Introduction

Journalism is a profession that hunts out trouble.

—Arab adage

THE EMERGENCE OF ARAB SATELLITE CHANNELS, notably Al Jazeera, has been the center of attention of western media and audiences, particularly for their war coverage beginning in Afghanistan and continuing in Iraq, for this is the first time that war has been seen "through Arab eyes" (Poniwozik, 2003:68). American and Arab news people agree that Arab satellite television channels are now one of the main sources of information in the Arab world, challenging American media hegemony (Sharkey, 2003). This has marked a change in the flow of information—conventionally said to be from the West to the East—from the East to the West (Hafez, 2002:121).

Different conclusions have been offered about the objectivity of war coverage by American versus Arab media. War coverage in the Arab media has been characterized as controversial, having adopted a perspective that is starkly different than that of the American media. The controversial reporting of Al Jazeera since September 11, 2001, for example, has been met with resentment in both the United States and the Middle East. Several Arab countries have expressed their resentment of the debates aired by the channel on issues deemed sensitive to their regimes. Indeed, the amount of attention directed at Al Jazeera is out of all proportion to the size of its tiny emirate host.[1] The difference in covering the recent war has been manifested in the Arab channels' choice of reporting on the war *on* Iraq, while the American media reported on

the war *in* Iraq. Al Jazeera, for one, was accused of giving space to Iraqi officials during the first weeks of the war, besides airing Saddam Hussein's tapes
and speeches. And while antiwar voices have received lots of attention on Al
Jazeera, pro-war voices were claimed to have received little or no coverage
(Reynolds, 2003). In other words, news reporting on Al Jazeera has been
deemed biased, albeit the same type of bias of some American networks
(Urbina, 2002).

Likewise, Arab media have magnified the political implications embraced
in the western—particularly American—media coverage of the recent war.
American media have been accused of twisting facts to favorably represent the
stance of their government. For example, a photo sent by the Associated Press
featuring an elderly Iraqi woman raising her hands with a caption saying she
was welcoming the American forces (or occupiers, as some Arab news media
choose to call them) has been interpreted differently by an Arab commentator, who saw in the woman's disturbed look and the position of her hands a
clear indication that she was in fact cursing, not welcoming, the Americans
(Amimour, 2003). While American (and western) media ridiculed the former
Iraqi Minister of Information As-Sahhaf, Arab journalists were criticizing the
"embedded war journalism" that was seen only to "cheer and clap for
the Anglo-American troops."[2] American journalists and scholars alike have
also criticized their media coverage, accusing it of abandoning the ethic of objectivity and embracing the principle of patriotism , thus giving in to the public opinion of the moment.[3]

Scrutinizing media coverage in both spheres, although a worthy exercise per
se, shows only reactions on the surface but does not go deeper than that. Assuming that news is a "form of culture" (Schudson, 1995:3), then interpreting
what is reported at a certain moment only in light of how different it is from
"our" reporting may lead to misleading conclusions, for it disregards the general
and specific factors that define the news in that particular culture. News values
in the Arab media have not received much attention from media scholars, except for a few studies (Abu Bakr, 1980; Turkistani, 1989; Nasser, 1983) that
might be outdated by now given ongoing developments on the Arab media
scene. An up-to-date scholarly examination of this topic is needed more than
ever, when the main sources of analysis have been journalists and individual observers. There have been, however, several studies on the symbolic features of
the news, for example stereotypes or images (Kamalipour, 1995; Wolfsfeld et al.,
2002; Diamond, 2002; Said, 1997), while social determinants, such as journalists' view of their role, the relationship between political and cultural environ-
ments, and news manufacturing, have been underrepresented.[4]

This book is a modest contribution on the long research road of examining
the components of the news media in the Arab region. Its main focus is on

Arab news values and how they are manifested textually in the news. The book argues that news values in the Arab media share some characteristics with the news values known from the American news media. These similarities, however, are still confined to the news form (i.e., news genre and format) and this is probably due to the professional level of the new generation of journalists. This new development, which the Arab news media has witnessed, cannot only be interpreted in terms of media globalization as an external force. Rather, the change has been made possible due to national, organizational, and professional changes in the media context within the region itself. At the national level, some Arab countries have witnessed political reforms accompanying changing regimes, either as a direct result of generation change or in seeking a new image for these countries. At the organizational level, news media outlets have managed to adjust to the new changes and use them as a sign of modernization in their institutions. Professionally, a new generation of western-trained and -educated Arab journalists has emerged and has occupied the leading positions in the newly established media outlets. In their attempt to modernize both their profession and their media output, both journalists and media institutions alike seek their inspiration from the developed world, particularly the United States. Also, journalism and media education in the Arab world usually adopts materials translated from English, due in part to the lack of locally produced materials and theories (Abu Bakr, 1985; Abdel Rahman, 1991; Al Jammal, 2001). All these factors have combined to contribute to the changes currently taking place on the Arab media scene. However, this book does not adhere to the optimistic theory that sees these changes as inevitably precipitating a democratization of the Arab world. The notion that the news format and heated political debates will eventually lead to the democratization of the region is rather dubious, perhaps because the same factor that has led to the mounting popularity of the news media, namely their regionalization, is the same factor that diminishes their political impact. The news media outlets are in harsh competition to attract more regional audiences, and consequently they are forced to prioritize foreign policy and inter-relational issues at the expense of more immediate, internal problems, which differ from country to country.

The aim of this book is to shed light on the current news values in the Arab news media as formulated by Arab and western scholars and observers alike, thus ensuring the presentation of input from both sides, rather than interpreting the news values solely from a western theoretical angle. To emphasize the frame of these values, a comparative approach is adopted, relating Arab news values to American news values. In addition, the values discussed will not only be revealed from a social and political point of view but also textually: that is, how they are manifested in the news text itself. Thus, the contribution of this study is twofold: it adopts the comparative approach needed for current media research (Schudson, 2003:7; Golding & Elliott, 1979), and it converges two fields, language analysis and social science, which should otherwise complement each other (Geis, 1987).

Global Convergence

Jenkins (2001:93) defines the media convergence as comprising a number of convergence processes, among them "global convergence," just as pressures from the World Bank and International Monetary Fund have further facilitated the deregulation of the media sector (Hafez, 2001:8). This process is defined as "the cultural hybridity that results from the international circulation of media content" (Jenkins, 2001:93). This form of cultural hybridity is present in the Arab region, to which American cultural products have been flowing alongside locally manufactured cultural products, such as Egyptian and Lebanese, which have succeeded in incorporating western (American) popular aspects into the Oriental fabric. The popularity and professionalism associated with American cultural products have been both the cause and effect of the cultural convergence, which is marked now in the Arab media. Syndicated programs, particularly *Who Wants to Be a Millionaire*, have been among the most popular programs on Arab television channels.[5] The sitcom *Friends* now has an Arabic version called *Shabab Online*, or *Youth Online* (Stanley, 2003). Arab audiences have been introduced to diverse American genres, not to mention other forms of culture, such as the several fast-food chains in the Arab region.

Several Arab scholars have pointed to the genre of music videos as the place where this convergence is negatively demonstrated. An Emirate researcher, for instance, states that "video clips" contribute to the marginalization of the Arab woman. In her paper to a conference on media and gender, held in Amman, Amina Al Dhaheri (2000) discussed the role of video clips on the presentation of Arab women. She examined fourteen songs of Arab singers from the Gulf region. The results showed that women in these videos were more likely to have foreign (Caucasian) features and be dressed in western style (jeans or lightly dressed). In addition, Sensenig-Dabbous (2000:15) argues that Lebanese youth are subjected to contradicting messages in media products that seem to depict a different society than the one they live in. For instance, sexual promiscuity is allowed on the screen, while civil laws, together with inherited morals and traditions, prohibit it.

The convergence is not only seen in the importation of western music and entertainment genres but also in the development of the news genre in the Arab media and the development of television journalism, which is said to have been non-existent in Arab world television. Ayish (2001a) conducted a quantitative analysis of a five-day sample of newscasts on five Arab satellite channels representing diverse political orientations.[6] His findings point to the increasing technical quality of the newscasts on these channels, demonstrated in the composition of a series of news intros and reports accompanied by a video and live reporting. One reason for this turn was to attract audiences that had been attracted to the CNN format, particularly during the 1991 Gulf War. Nevertheless, some satellite channels, particularly those categorized as "traditional" (Ayish, 2002b), still adhere to the traditional news format, with its poor technical quality. The Syrian satellite channel, for instance, prefers to draw on voiceovers and on-camera items (Ayish, 2001a). The news genre in the emerged Arab satellite channels thus shares two main characteristics with American television news: sensationalism and technical quality. Also, several political talk shows are modeled on the American format. For example, *Crossfire* has an Arabic version on Al Jazeera, *The Opposite Direction* (al-Kasim, 1999). In fact, Khouri (2001) claims that the Arab news media have managed to combine the worst of both worlds: the sensational and confrontational style of American media with the Arab tradition of "absolutist" debate. Arab satellite channels are also said to be under the CNN-effect that was demonstrated during the 1991 Gulf War, allocating more time to live battlefield coverage (Adwan, 2003).

Thus, while the Americanization of certain (serious) genres, such as news and debate programs, has been hailed as a sign of a progressive and democratic revolution in the region, the Americanization of the (popular) genres, such as music videos and soap operas, has been regarded as a regression from the authentic heritage of the region, as diagramed in figure I.1.

There are a number of factors that have facilitated this convergence. One of them is the emergence of a new generation of Arab journalists, who have either received a large part of their education and training in western media institutions or have been educated in western-oriented schools and colleges in their home countries (Sakr, 2001:124f). Previous research among Arab journalists points to the fact that the majority of them hold university degrees, usually at the B.A. level (Abdel Rahman, 1989; Kirat, 1987; Tash, 1983). Another study, which dealt with the working situation of journalists in Lebanese television, confirmed this result (Al Kadry & Harb, 2002).[7] The new generation of western-oriented and -trained journalists is deemed an important catalyst to the introduction of new genres, for example political debates and talk shows, and more sophisticated interview techniques, previously unpracticed by the Arab media (Ayish, 2001a).

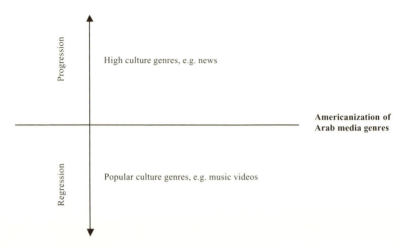

Figure I.1   Americanization of Arab Media Genres

Another factor is the external competition the Arab media face at the moment. Drawing on its popularity during the 1991 Gulf War, CNN launched a website in Arabic, and several media outlets have followed suit. CNBC Arabiya, for instance, was inaugurated on July 27, 2003 (Davies, 2003). The external competition is said to add pressure on Arab governments to release their grip on television content and allow new programming techniques (Ayish, 1995). Arabic service on foreign radio stations, particularly the BBC, Radio Monte Carlo, and Voice of America (VOA), has been very popular and has been regarded as the main source of news unauthorized by the traditional Arab media. It is not unusual to tune in to one of these stations to find out what is happening in one's own country,[8] particularly during the wars (Ghareeb, 2000). Audience analyses conducted among Arab listeners during the 1980s showed a clear pattern of these stations' popularity among Arab publics (Ayish, 1991). Needless to say, the same stations were again the main source of news during the 1991 Gulf War. The external competition has also forced Arab media policymakers to launch foreign language channels; for example, the Egyptian and Syrian satellite channels air programs in Hebrew.[9] The news media initiated by foreign countries outside the region, such as the American-sponsored Sawa Radio, constitute one immediate challenge for Arab media policymakers who might find themselves in a dilemma: on one hand, they feel obliged to allow for the establishment of these media outlets to show their goodwill in establishing a common channel of dialogue among their countries and the United States, and on the other hand, they find it difficult to apply rigid rules prohibiting foreign ownership of the news media (Ghareeb, 2000).

Scholars (Ghareeb, 2000; Ayish, 2002b) agree that the 1991 Gulf War was the catalyst needed to initiate media reforms in the Arab region, which, among others, included the establishment of several satellite channels, notably MBC, ART, and Orbit (Saudi Arabia); Al Jazeera (Qatar); LBCI (Lebanon); ESC (Egypt); Abu Dhabi and Dubai (Emirates); and RTM (Morocco). MBC was established in 1991 by wealthy Saudis related to the royal family. Then in 1993, ART was established in Rome with funds from one of the MBC founders, and the Moroccan RTM followed suit in 1994. Italy had been the base for another Arab satellite adventure, namely Orbit, also Saudi owned, established in 1994. Orbit entered a joint agreement with the Arabic service of the BBC to launch an Arabic television news service, but the project did not last long after the new BBC channel decided to air a program with Saudi opposition guests. The Lebanese LBC was launched in 1985 during the civil war as a terrestrial channel, and by the end of the war it began broadcasting via satellite. Although the channel launched a number of news programs that provoked political debate, pushing the government to exercise their censorship powers and the channel to challenge it in court, LBC is more known for its cultural and entertainment productions. This in turn has secured the channel the highest advertising revenues among Arab satellite channels.[10] Al Jazeera, launched in 1996, has become one of the most popular news channels. Most of Al Jazeera's staff worked on the short-lived joint venture between the BBC and Orbit. In 2000, the Abu Dhabi channel emerged as a professional news and entertainment provider, employing around 650 people. The channel has three main, important advantages that distinguish it from other regional players: financial support, the newest technology, and a reasonable amount of journalistic freedom (Ghareeb, 2000). In addition, the Al-Arabiya satellite channel was launched recently by the Middle East Broadcasting Center as a rival to Al Jazeera.

There is fierce competition among the Arab satellite channels, to the benefit of the audiences (Hafez, 2001). The Arab world has also experienced the first media merging venture in the cooperative agreement between the Lebanese LBC channel and the pan-Arab newspaper *Al Hayat*, whose professional political coverage the former will use. The chief editor of *Al Hayat*, Jihad Khazen, has even confirmed that the success of this venture might lead to an LBC/*Al Hayat* 24-hour news channel.[11] Arab channels, both terrestrial and satellite, have joined the fray, spreading new genres, including political talk shows. One successful host of a political talk show, Hamdi Qandil, whose program centered on foreign policy issues like the Israeli–Palestinian conflict, admits that satellite channels have paved the way for the spread of

such shows. Most importantly, Arab authorities now realize that what the audience needs is serious programs and not just entertainment (Elbendary,
2001).

The emergence of new media outlets in the Arab region has contributed to
the regionalization of the political debate, although access to these media has
initially been limited to the elites. The new media can be characterized by the
fact that they not only address Arab audiences in the region but also reach a
wider audience among Arabs in Europe and the Americas (Ghareeb, 2000;
Alterman, 1998). The dominance of Saudi Arabia via its ownership of several
satellite channels and pan-Arab newspapers adds to the country's regional
cultural and economic power. Saudi Arabia represents a lucrative market for
cultural imports from other Arab countries, particularly Egypt (Hafez,
2001:8f), and it is the most important advertiser (Khazen, 1999). As the most
important customer, the Saudi Arabian market enforces a number of restrictions on the flow of publications and cultural products into the country:
kisses and drinks, for example, may not be shown. Critics refer to this rigid
attitude and its effect on the Arab regional market as the "bedouinization of
Arab culture" (Hafez, 2001:8f). This is rather a paradox, considering that the
majority of the new satellite channels are actually owned by Saudi business
tycoons and that the abundance of musical shows featuring semi-nude
women on several of these channels does not correspond to the cultural heritage of their owners (Ayish, 2001b; al-Kasim, 1999). In fact, it is tempting to
divide the new satellite channels among those specializing in drama (Egyptian), those specializing in entertainment (Saudi and Lebanese), and those
specializing in news and serious political debates (Qatari and Saudi).

Out of fear of losing their grip on the control of media development in the
region, Jordan, Egypt, Lebanon, and the United Arab Emirates, recognizing
that if they cannot beat competitors, they had better join them, have established free media zones to host foreign and regional media institutions, granting them full operating freedom and total exemption from taxes and fees.
This, in turn, has been interpreted as a double-standard policy, which grants
more freedom to media outlets inside the free zones while prohibiting it for
journalists outside.[12] Dubai Media City, for one, serves 550 media organizations, among them CNN, Reuters, Sony, McGraw-Hill Publishing, and the
Arab satellite channel MBC (Chaker, 2003).

Moreover, a new generation of Arab leaders has claimed political power in
Syria, Jordan, Morocco, and Qatar, and has initiated a number of reforms to
differentiate their modern, western-oriented thinking from that of the former
regimes (Alterman, 2002). The young Syrian President Bashar Al Assad has
expressed his interest in modernizing the Syrian media. One initiative was his
meeting with representatives of the Syrian Press Council to listen to their

problems. Since the appointment of a new minister of information in 2000, shortly before the death of former President Hafez Al Assad, the media sector has witnessed a number of improvements, including the issuing of licenses to forty private newspapers and four private, non-political radio stations, and allowing 350 foreign publications (including Arab) to be sold in Syria (*Al Hayat*, 2 October, 2003). The president has also initiated two directives breaking with the former press tradition under the rule of his father: one called on editors-in-chief to adopt a "calm, logical and balanced style," while the other prohibited the printing of the young president's picture and referring to him as "Al Raid al-Khalid" (the immortal one).[13]

Jordanian King Abdallah II, who assumed the throne in 1999 following the death of King Hussein, introduced several amendments to the press laws to ensure more media freedom, including removal of the restrictions imposed by the 1993 press law and a reduction of the capital requirement to launch a newspaper. He has also granted journalists access to government information. Other restrictions, however, have not been changed. For example, the requirement that all journalists are members of the Journalists' Union, or the ban on reporting secret sessions of Parliament. In October 2001, King Abdallah II abolished the Ministry of Information and replaced it with the Higher Media Council, consisting of eleven members responsible for recommending media policy and answering directly to the king.[14]

After Moroccan King Mohamed VI claimed the throne in 1999, the new press law of 2002 reduced the prison penalty for newsmen who denigrate a government official or a member of the royal family. Nevertheless, the penalties are still harsh and the authorities still have the right to revoke a license or censor publications if they are deemed to threaten the national security.[15] King Mohamed VI promised a more open media policy to contribute to Morocco's development, including opening the information sector to freedom of speech, while respecting the professional codes of ethics (www.arabicnews.com, 12 July 2002).

The establishment of the Al Jazeera channel followed the initiative of the young Emir of Qatar to mark his regime after his bloodless coup in 1995. He thought first of building an entertainment channel, following the example of the several Saudi wealthy men, but his advisers managed to convince him to establish a news channel instead. Although the governmental loan to Al Jazeera is supposed to end within five years of its establishment, the government is not expected to back off if the channel runs into financial trouble, for Al Jazeera has for the first time put Qatar on the map and given it greater regional influence (Ghareeb, 2000).

At the social level, there have been significant changes contributing to the success of this convergence, among them the importance of the English language in the Arab labor market. Modern Standard Arabic (MSA) is no longer in demand as an important qualification, particularly when more and more foreign corporations have established their presence in several Arab countries, imposing English as their lingua franca. With the unfortunate combination of an increasing number of young people and the increasing unemployment rate, Arab families have felt the need to send their children to English-language schools (if they can afford them), even if that undermines their proficiency in MSA[16] (Haeri, 1997; Howeidy, 1999). One outcome is naturally that larger and larger segments of the population can follow the news media in English[17] with little difficulty, and thus they become familiar not only with the news genres but also debate traditions in the foreign media.

The new, imported genres, particularly live political debates, and news formats might increase the audience's trust in the new media, besides familiarizing them with new traditions for political participation. It also contributes to increasing professionalism among Arab journalists. But without genuine change from within each nation, the change will remain at the symbolic level and the heated debates on the new channels will only be seen as "a safety valve to release public pressures and suppressions and a way to absorb the inherent conflicts" (Taweela, 2002:4) similar to the harsh tone used by the traditional media in the wake of the 1967 defeat. For foreign viewers, these debates might be interpreted as a step in the right direction toward democratization, but this could be far from true. It is like watching an Arab drama or music video featuring an extravagant life that can by no means be a reflection of the average Arab (Taweela, 2002; Sensenig-Dabbous, 2000). Likewise, reading the economic and business sections in several Arab newspapers, as an Arab media scholar (Abdel Nabi, 1989) said, would give the mistaken impression that Arabs live a luxurious life because the media tend to focus on the life of urban, well-educated, upper-middle-class citizens rather than addressing the average citizen's problems, particularly in the countryside, where the majority still live. This is probably why scholars do not agree on the functional perspectives of the current development, and there are two lines of thinking: integrationist and fragmentationist (Ayish, 2002a). Adherents of the integrationist role of media argue that the new media will contribute to the formation of pan-Arab visions and goals, not to mention a common cultural identity. Fragmentationists argue that television has lost its role, presenting a cultural chaos that ultimately will force the Arab publics to seek alternative cultural identities.

The above factors contribute to the continuous development of the Arab news media in order to attract regional audiences. Figure I.2 shows the convergence of interests of the above actors and factors.

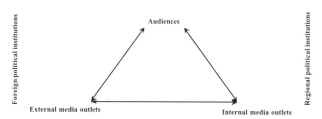

Figure I.2   Factors Influencing the Development of Arab News Media

The regional media outlets compete to attract regional audiences by offering new genres and daring talk shows. Audiences, in turn, have access to both regional and foreign media, even if the latter do not seek to "Arabize" their output, for example, CNBC Arabiya. Foreign news media include both Arabic-language services by foreign media—the BBC and VOA—and the media outlets initiated by political institutions, such as Radio Sawa, which seek to influence Arab public opinion. Moreover, regional political regimes exercise a form of pressure on the regional media partly by deregulating the media sector, thereby intensifying competition, and partly by controlling media output via legislation and administrative regulations. The competition between external and regional media outlets clearly results in increasing professionalism among newspeople.

What Follows

Believing that the Arab region is a homogeneous unit and that development of the news genre has gone through a unified process is a misconception. Naturally, there are several shared characteristics among Arab countries with regard to their media policies, but there are a number of differences among them as well. Chapter one compares and contrasts the Arab countries with regard to their media environment and policies. Then, chapter two will shed some light on the historical development of the news media in the Arab region to establish the context in which to place current regional developments.

Researchers have assigned several roles to the media: agenda setting, socialization, cultural change, and propaganda (McQuail, 2002:425ff). But the media may not have such great influence after all; it is also possible that public opinion affects media more than the media affects public opinion (Schudson, 2003:20). For example, Americans' support or rejection of the Vietnam War at the end of the 1960s was contrary to the news media's angle (Schudson,

2003:19f). In the wake of the recent Iraq war, several Arab media outlets claimed that most of them began the war coverage with an objective angle but soon followed the sensational wave of the satellite channels in an attempt to attract larger audiences (*Al Sharq Al Awsat*, 18 April 2003). The agenda-setting role of the Arab news media will be addressed in chapter three as a part of the general discussion and reevaluation of William Rugh's typology of Arab press.

In an attempt to emphasize their autonomy and detachment from the men in power, American journalists rely on (and sometimes overdo) the use of negative news, particularly that involving politicians (Schudson, 2003:98; Patterson, 1993). This trend is what other scholars have termed the "spiral of cynicism": Journalists tend to use the language of game, war, and conflict, framing the political news stories strategically and leading readers to attribute cynical motives (Cappella & Jamieson, 1997). The media's obsession with reporting on scandals and misdeeds rather than on positive accomplishments has one major drawback. What scholars fear is the increasing "tabloidization" of the news media, threatening the founding ethics of the journalistic profession (Schudson, 2003:90). Moreover, the credibility aspired to by all the news media in the United States and several western European countries has long been exacerbated by the newspeople's reliance on official sources in reporting political news. One study on the American cable channels' coverage of the recent war found that the majority of the news stories depended on the White House, Pentagon, and State Department for information on the war (Andrew Tyndall, reported in Cunningham, 2003). On the other hand, examining recent research on Arab news media—given the role of global convergence, albeit at the symbolic level—one can point to a number of values that characterize news selection in contemporary Arab news media: the significance of political news, the social responsibility carried in the selection process, objectivity, prominence and sensationalism, and newness. These values, similar to those in American media, will be the center of discussion in chapter four.

Part II begins with a general overview, in chapter five, of the development of news as a genre in the Arab press, shedding light on the characteristics of this particular genre. In the discussion of news values and how they are anchored in the social reality of the media in the Arab region, it is also imperative to draw on the language used by the news media, MSA. There is a diglossia in the Arab region between two varieties of languages: one written variety (MSA) for formal purposes, including news reporting, and the vernaculars, which differ from one country to another. Why MSA has been the preferred medium for news reporting and how news values are reflected textually via that medium will be the central issues discussed in chapters six and seven, respectively.

Finally, some concluding remarks will round out the discussion, with a brief evaluation of the effect of the Arab news media, particularly its so-called democratization process and whether this effect is overstated or well founded.

Notes

1. Egyptian President Mubarek was said to express his surprise at the size of the building hosting Al Jazeera in Qatar, by sarcastically asking, "All this noise comes from this matchbox?" (Zednik, Rick. Perspectives on war: Inside Al Jazeera. *Columbia Journalism Review*, 40, 6:44–47.)

2. Faisal Al Qassem, one of the prominent TV hosts at Al Jazeera, expressed that opinion in Janardhan, N. Media-Mideast: Arab Media under Fire for Anti-U.S. War Coverage. *Global Information Network*, 12 June 2003 (1).

3. In fact, MSNBC defended the principle of "patriotic" coverage by saying, "It's not inconsistent to say you are a patriotic American and a journalist. It's not inconsistent to say that you believe in our troops and want them to come home safely, and on the other hand, you're a reporter and it's your job to ask questions of everybody you meet and try to explore every angle of the story." Quoted in Sharkey, Jacqueline E. The television war. *American Journalism Review*, 25, 4:18.

4. Schudson (2003:183) differentiates between two understandings of the news production: 1) cultural views highlighting textual and structural elements in the news; and 2) social-organizational views that reveal the results of interaction among various players in the news production process, such as ownership, market, and laws.

5. In fact, the program has been very popular in the Gulf countries, where 80 percent of audiences in Saudi Arabia and the Emirates follow it, not to mention its popularity in other countries, such as Yemen. Yemenis have even complained to the MBC because only a few Yemenis have appeared on the program as contestants. Consequently, and to maintain this popularity, MBC felt the need to move the program from its studios in London to an Arab capital to facilitate the participation of contestants from all over the region (Source: *Al Sharq Al Awsat*, 2 March 2001).

6. These channels were Abu Dhabi Satellite Channel (Emirates), Al Jazeera (Qatar), MBC (Saudi Arabia), LBC (Lebanon), and the Syrian Satellite Channel (Syria). The sample included nightly newscasts from these channels taken over five days in 2000.

7. In fact, the main aim of this research was to compare the working conditions of men versus women journalists at these stations. The authors showed that women journalists have higher educational degrees and more qualifications, such as mastering foreign languages, than their male colleagues.

8. Al-Kasim (1999) adds sarcastically that one Syrian comedian used to say that he tuned in to London to find out what was happening in Syria.

9. www.aljazeera.net/cases_analysis/2003/8/8-24-1.htm (12 January 2004).

10. Out of the US$150 million of advertising revenues of satellite channels in 2000, the share of LBC and Future TV (both are Lebanese) was 48 percent, compared to only 35 percent for MBC. www.lebanonadvisor.com/downloads/pdf/english/business_chap3.pdf (12 January 2004).

11. Interview with Jihad Khazen. www.tbsjournal.com/Archives/Fall02/LBC.html (23 January 2004).

12. The Stanhope Centre for Communications Policy Research (2003): Study of Media Laws and policies for the Middle East and Maghrib, p. 24f. Available at: www.internews.org/arab_media_research

13. The Stanhope Centre for Communications Policy Research (2003). Report on Syrian media policy. www.internews.org/arab_media_research-Syria file, page 2 (12 January 2004).

14. See www.internews.org/arab_media_research/jordan.pdf (12 January 2004).

15. See www.cpj.org/attacks02/arabic/morocco_arab.html (15 March 2004).

16. MSA is the written variety of Arabic that is confined to formal correspondence. For more detail about the role of MSA and the existence of vernacular and written forms, see chapters six and seven.

17. In fact, according to Yamani (2000), young Saudis tend to watch a range of channels, including CNN, even if they do not speak English.

I

1

The Arab Region: Similarities and Differences

Language is bound to remain the mainspring of cultural identity, and linguistic diversity the mainspring of all other diversities.

—Amin Maalouf, *On Identity*

THE REASON WHY THE ARAB region is classified as such probably is not due to the spread of Islam as the major religion, but rather to the spread of Arabic as the main language. A Moroccan and a Yemeni will regard each other as Arabs, but their favorite daily newspaper or television program might be from a third country in the region. The region shares a common media language, Modern Standard Arabic (MSA) although some scholars note that the level of Arabic used in the media is different from MSA (Cantarino, 1974–76; Holes, 1995). The sharing of one common language, albeit a language that is used for written communication and not daily contact, has facilitated the spread of publications and media messages among these countries (Abu Bakr et al., 1985).

Despite the existence of one media language, each Arab country has developed a distinctive dialect. Needless to say, in each country several sub-dialects also exist, such as urban and rural. As Clive Holes (1995) put it,

The greater the distance between any two points of comparison, by and large, the greater will be the differences between the ordinary vernaculars spoken in them. It is not then surprising to find that the varieties of Arabic spoken at the extreme peripheries of the area differ from each other considerably, and certainly to the point of mutual unintelligibility if we were to compare what might be called the plain uneducated vernaculars—say that of an Omani nomad with that of a Moroccan townsman from Marrakech. (3)

The spread of Islam accompanied, if not caused, the spread of the Arabic language in the region. Arabic, the language of the Koran, is different from the MSA used by Arab literates and the media (Holes, 1995:11ff). Other factors contributing to the spread of Arabic were the migration of people from Arabia to other parts of the region, together with the continuous urbanization of areas where the Arab conquerors resided. The latter factor meant, though, that the peasant areas managed to keep indigenous languages like Coptic, Aramaic, and Greek, if not as the official language, then at least side by side with Arabic.

Despite the unifying force of the Arabic language,[1] it is remarkable that there is no single, clear-cut term to describe the Arab identity: Arab, Arabic, Arabian all exist in the language and are sometimes used interchangeably to describe a person or thing stemming from the region. The phrase "Middle East" is, as Sreberny-Mohammadi (1998:180) points out, "a geo-political label given to a region by western powers after the First World War," and it "should not lead to assumptions about similarities between these countries." Hussein Amin (2001:23) defines the Arab world as the following countries: Algeria, Bahrain, Egypt, Iraq, Jordan, Kuwait, Lebanon, Libya, Morocco, Oman, Palestine, Qatar, Saudi Arabia, Sudan, Syria, Tunisia, The United Arab Emirates, and Yemen. Abu Bakr (1985:20) points to the possibility of dividing the Arab countries in three communities based on geopolitical considerations: North Africa (Libya, Tunisia, Morocco, and Algeria); the Nile Valley (Sudan and Egypt); and Asian-Arab countries or the Levant (Syria, Lebanon, Jordan, and Palestine, the Gulf, and the Arabian Peninsula).[2]

There are striking differences among these countries in terms of economic indicators and political policies, not to mention the size of their populations. The United Arab Emirates had the highest per capita Gross National Product (GNP) in 1996, US$17,400, while Yemen had the lowest GNP, US$260 (United Nations Education, Scientific and Cultural Organization [UNESCO], 1999–2000). Likewise, Egypt had a population estimated at 66 million in 1996, compared to Qatar's 0.54 million in the same year (Sreberny-Mohammadi, 1998:182). Also, the type of political regime differs among the countries. Seven of the nineteen countries have monarchies, which range from traditional to constitutional, while several other countries are republics.

According to a 2004 assessment by the American organization Freedom House, the Arab countries are far behind others in political rights and civil liberties. Table 1.1, which ranks Arab countries according to the degree of freedom enjoyed, is extracted from the General World Index.[3]

Table 1.1   **Freedom Index of Arab Countries**

| 0–30 = Free, 31–60 = Partly Free, 61–100 = Not Free | | |
Country	Index	Degree of freedom
Kuwait	57	Partly Free
Qatar	61	Not Free
Morocco	61	Not free
Jordan	63	Not Free
Algeria	63	Not Free
Lebanon	66	Not Free
Iraq	66	Not Free
Yemen	67	Not Free
Bahrain	70	Not Free
Oman	74	Not Free
United Arab Emirates	75	Not Free
Egypt	76	Not Free
Tunisia	80	Not Free
Syria	80	Not Free
Saudi Arabia	80	Not Free
Sudan	85	Not Free
Palestinian Authority	86	Not Free
Libya	94	Not Free

Source: Adapted from the Freedom House report 2004, www.freedomhouse.org.

The score of Qatar (not free) seems to contradict the image this small emirate is trying to project of itself as host of the controversial Al Jazeera satellite channel, airing debates about issues sensitive to several Arab regimes. In contrast, the United States scored thirteen in the same survey, thus placing it among the "free" countries. As the table shows, none of the seventeen Arab countries belong to the "free" part of the world, although Kuwait was placed among the "partly free" countries.

The United Nations Development Program's (UNDP) Human Development Index (HDI) supports this conclusion by asserting that "out of seven world regions, the Arab countries had the lowest freedom score in the late 1990s" (7). The report concludes that "the range of disparity among Arab countries on the HDI is almost as wide as that observed in the entire world" (UNDP, 2002:27). It added that among the main obstacles to the very necessary cooperation among the Arab states are the desire of most of them to imitate other economic groups like the European Union without taking into account the differences among them and the differences in the political regimes. That Arab states cooperate has been one general recommendation for the economic development of the region because of the disparity of human and natural resources among the Arab countries—some countries require enormous resources but lack the money, while others have the financial resources but lack qualified human resources (Abu Bakr et al., 1985). Cooperation in the field of communications, although one of the priorities of the Arab League Educational, Cultural, and Scientific Organization (ALESCO), has been constrained by the difference in the amount of freedom in the Arab states, sanctions applied, and the different media policies adopted in each state, as discussed below.

Literacy is a prerequisite for the public's access to the print news media and the literacy rate in the Arab region is low. According to the 2000–2004 UNESCO survey, literacy ranges from 49 percent to 90 percent, with the literacy rate of men higher than that of women, as illustrated in table 1.2.

The lower illiteracy rate in Lebanon is reflected in the number of dailies and magazines registered in the country in 1995; at 101 dailies, the country has the highest number of newspapers in the region, compared to only one in Yemen. On the other hand, the high illiteracy rate in Egypt does not correspond directly to the number of publications in the country, which is 53, among which there are 15 dailies, although the circulation per 1,000 inhabitants was only 38 in the same period. As will be discussed later, both Lebanon and Egypt can be considered veterans in the information and communications industry. Abdelfattah (1990:36f) notices the correlation between literacy and newspaper readership in Egypt, particularly from the beginning of the twentieth

Table 1.2   Literacy Rate in Arab Countries, 2000–2004

Country	Adult literacy as %			Youth literacy rate as %		
	Total	Male	Female	Total	Female	Male
Egypt	55.6	67.2 (63.6)*	43.6 (38.8)	73.2	79.0	66.9
Qatar	84.2	84.9 (79.2)	82.3 (79.9)	94.8	94.1	95.8
Syria	82.9	91.0 (85.7)	74.2 (55.8)	95.2	97.1	93.0
Algeria	68.9	78.0 (73.9)	59.6 (49.1)	89.9	94.0	85.6
Bahrain	88.5	91.5 (89.1)	84.2 (79.4)	98.6	98.4	98.9
Jordan	90.0	95.5 (82.2)	85.9 (79.4)	99.4	99.3	99.5
Kuwait	82.9	84.7 (82.2)	81.0 (74.9)	93.1	92.2	93.9
Libya	81.7	91.8 (87.9)	70.7 (63.1)	97.0	99.8	94.0
Morocco	50.7	63.3 (56.6)	38.3 (31)	69.5	77.4	61.3
Oman	74.4	82.0 (71)	65.4 (46)	98.5	99.6	97.3
Saudi Arabia	77.9	84.1 (71.5)	69.5 (50.3)	93.5	95.4	91.6
Sudan	59.9	70.8 (57.7)	49.1 (34.6)	79.1	83.9	74.2
Tunisia	73.2	83.1 (78.6)	63.1 (54.6)	94.3	97.9	90.6
UAE	77.3	75.6 (78.9)	80.7 (79.8)	91.4	88.2	95.0
Yemen	49.0	69.5 (39)	28.5	67.9	84.3	50.9
Iraq	NA	(70.7)	(45)			

Source: Adapted from UNESCO Institute for Statistics, 2000–2004.
* Figures in parentheses adapted from UNESCO World Communication and Information Report: Arab Countries 1999–2000.

century until 1980. Amin (2001:24) confirms this tendency and points out that the higher the literacy in a given population, the higher the newspaper circulation. Therefore, newspaper circulation is rather limited in the region due to the high illiteracy rate.

Income is another parameter that influences newspaper readership: the higher the income, the higher the access to print media. Among low-income individuals, electronic media are preferred as the main source of information and entertainment (Abdelfattah, 1990:39). In Lebanon, for instance, audience analysis shows that the elite's consumption of print media far exceeds that of the working class (Dajani, 1992). Also, elite groups are inclined to watch foreign media, while working class groups prefer local programs. Dajani (1992) justifies this by noting that elite groups are more information-oriented and therefore prefer the traditional print media, while workers are more entertainment-oriented and therefore prefer electronic media.

According to UNESCO statistics, the number of newspapers and publications in the Arab world as a whole constitutes a fraction of the total world number, as shown in table 1.3.

Arabs' access to print as well as electronic media can be tabularized as illustrated in table 1.4.

There are no homogeneous media policies in the Arab region. In fact, Al Jammal (2001:14) argues that there are as many communications systems as there are Arab countries, and it is therefore wrong to generalize situations in one Arab country to the whole Arab world, although there are some similarities. One of the differences is in Arab countries' attitudes toward the right to free speech (Al Jammal:35ff). In 1970, the Arab League assigned a committee of experts to formulate a convention on human rights for the Arab world. Researchers found that the convention text was a copy of what the international conventions on human rights already included, although efforts were made to formulate the text to meet the acceptance of the majority of Arab countries. Yet only nine countries accepted the convention and the rest never replied. Some

Table 1.3   Arab Dailies

Year	# of dailies	Circulation (in millions)	Per 1,000 inhabitants	Of world total in %
1975	108	3.0	22	1.4
1985	125	6.4	32	1.48
1996	140	9.2	36	1.66

Source: UNESCO: Culture and Communication Statistics, http://portal.unesco.org/uis/TEMPLATE/html/Cult
AndCom/Table_IV_S_1.html.

Table 1.4   Arab Access to Media

Country	Radio receivers	TV receivers	# dailies (Per 1,000 inhabitants)	Circulation in 1000	Distribution
Yemen	43	267	3	230	15
Libya	213	138	4	71	13
Iraq	224	74	4	530	26
Syria	264	89	8	274	19
Bahrain	575	439	3	70	126
Palestine	n/a	n/a	n/a	n/a	n/a
Qatar	438	457	4	80	146
Algeria	238	71	8	1440	51
Jordan	251	175	4	250	47
Oman	580	61	4	63	28
Sudan	270	86	5	650	24
Tunisia	200	156	8	270	30
Morocco	226	145	20	630	24
UAE	271	263	8	310	140
Kuwait	473	373	9	655	387
Egypt	312	126	15	2,373	38
Saudi Arabia	291	269	12	1,060	58
Lebanon	891	268	14	330	110

Source: UNESCO, World Communication and Information Report 1999–2000.

other countries rejected the text categorically, and others suggested some modifications. Thus, differences among the Arab countries' ideas of human rights proved too serious for a joint effort in this direction. Some scholars argue that Arab countries cannot blindly adopt the western conception of democracy. Others argue that the solution is in pure Islamic values, while others justify the problem with the special heritage of the area—with centuries of colonialism and the absence of democracy. Finally, there are scholars who believe that the disagreement among Arab scholars is the real reason for the absence of democracy. The different interpretation of freedom and human rights among Arab states has two implications: Firstly, it has an effect upon the degree of tolerance allowed in media messages (both in serious genres such as news as well as popular culture). Secondly and more generally, there exist different laws and regulations covering most fields, including media. Having said that, it is important to recall that even among western democracies, there is not a unanimous interpretation of human rights. Thus, while the death penalty is seen as a sign of justice in several American states, several European countries condemn it on the basis that it violates the European conception of human rights.

Another difference among Arab nations can be found in the degree of correspondence required between media policies and general national policies. In addition, media policies are usually enforced by national laws, which differ from one country to another, and journalists' access to unions also differs from one country to another. Finally, there are different ethical codes governing the journalistic profession. Such ethical codes are usually found in the Arab countries that have longer experience in the media field and the professional organization of media people.

On the other hand, there are some similarities among Arab countries' communications and media policies (Al Jammal, 2001:49ff). First, these policies have never been integrated into general development policies and were not prioritized, as they should be. This is reflected in decreasing investment in this sector, especially in the field of production, so the countries are dependent on imported cultural products. Second, none of the Arab countries has had success in transforming its communications policies into long-term plans. Third, there is a common lack of audience and communications research, which should be the basis for any successful communications policy. In addition, existing communications policies serve mobilization purposes for the political regimes. As governmental administration is usually centered in the capital, so are the media institutions. In this respect, the media is used as a tool for preserving the status quo, politically and culturally, and is rarely used to change existing values. The media is seen as a tool of unification, fostering the spirit of one nation and undermining regional differences.

Despite similarities among Arab states, their efforts to launch mutual cooperation projects, particularly in the media field, have not been successful. Abdel Rahman (1989:153f) notes a number of obstacles that hinder such cooperation. Among these are the huge gap between poor and rich, or those who control the resources and policies and those who merely follow, and the authorities' attempts to co-opt the small group of intellectuals into serving their interests. In addition, the governments' direct and indirect monopoly of the media, not to mention cultural and media dependence on western sources, constitute barriers to cooperation. Thus, the road to mutual cooperation begins with each state attempting to initiate harmonizing plans on both the social and political levels.

Notes

1. Naturally, the presence of one "formal" language, MSA, has promoted a belief in Arab nationalism based on language rather than religion, thus embracing non-Muslim minorities. Nonetheless, there are different interpretations of the role of language in national identity (particularly in Egypt and Lebanon) and whether vernacular or MSA

should be the reflection of this identity. See, for example, Suleiman (2003) for a more detailed discussion of the role of language in Arab national identity.

2. Abu Bakr added to his classifications countries like Mauritania, Somalia, and Djibouti, but they are not included among Arab countries in this study.

3. Freedom House, 2004, www.freedomhouse.org.

2

History of Arab News

The Arabs had been so beaten down over the decades by their own auto-
cratic leaders, by their inability to manifest their sense of pan-Arab unity,
by their inability to do anything about Israel, by their inability to forge pro-
ductive and honorable relations with the great powers, that they had hit
rock bottom.

—Rami Khouri, *The Gulf War: An Arab Perspective*

DURING THE AMERICAN COLONIAL PERIOD, publishers were subject to the
crown's licensing power, not to mention the risk of prison if they offended the authorities. Even after the end of licensing, the penalties continued
to control the newspapermen's work. The press then took on a political role
that was further enforced by the emergence of the partisan press by the end of
eighteenth century. Later, the year 1833 witnessed an important breakthrough
in American journalism with the launching of the *New York Sun* as the first
penny press, aiming at readers with modest incomes. Advertising was particularly welcomed to enforce the papers' independence from party subsidies
(Kilmer, 2002). The reasons behind the emergence of the penny press are still
unclear, whether it was the high literacy rate, the advanced technology, the
emergence of the bourgeoisie, new journalistic innovations, or a combination
of all these. Commercialization gave advertisers an economic power to impose
a new kind of news writing, where advertising was subtly blended into the
news stories. Now, newspaper ownership has been consolidated in the hands of
powerful chains and groups (Claussen, 2002). Yet, profit is not the driving force
behind the launching of newspapers; publishers may establish a newspaper to

ensure a platform for their political opinions, although it is claimed that this does necessarily influence the news content (Schudson, 2003:118).

Since its dawn, Arab news media were related to politics (McFadden, 1953). Unlike American news media, Arab media had neither undergone a commercialization process nor the emergence of a strong bourgeoisie. Yet, commercialization is not the sole prerequisite for professional journalism or press freedom. There are several media systems in Europe, including the so-called public service media, where the subsidy of media institutions comes from the state. Nonetheless, these media systems have developed high journalistic standards and secured access to pluralistic opinion.[1]

Because news values are the product of the political, social, and economic environment in which the news media operate, it is imperative to analyze them in this context. The aim of this chapter is to shed some light, albeit briefly, on the historical development of the news media in the Arab world. Because the printing press was the first mass communications means, its role will be discussed in more detail both in this chapter and the next one. This chapter seeks to address the development process of the news media, beginning from the eighteenth century and going through the different stages and the roles filled by the media. Another factor in this development is the various forms of pressure on the news media, such as the laws and penalties Arab regimes have sought to impose. In this respect, the chapter will also seek to address the problem of self-censorship as a direct result of political and administrative pressures and as an indirect result of market pressure.

Arab media policymakers were keen to establish national news agencies as a means of controlling the flow of information from the West to the East. Their efforts, however, to establish a joint Arab news agency have not been successful. This chapter will shed light on the role of the national news agencies as gatekeepers.

From Interpersonal to Mass Communication

Poetry was regarded as one important means of communication in the Arab world prior to the Islamic era (Tash, 1983:32). It was used as a means of informing people on the Arabian Peninsula about the achievements of tribes and the defeat of their enemies. Thus, it played a major role as a mobilization and propaganda instrument. After the arrival of Islam, new means were adopted, for example the *imam* (preachers) in the mosques, who orally communicated with the congregation on various issues during Friday services (Ayalon, 1995:4f). The imam in the mosque and *munadi* (town criers), played a role in disseminating information and communicating important messages from the authorities to the people (Ayalon, 1995:6). Formal communication in the Islamic empire was seen to serve one main function, "to promote and inculcate the Islamic way of life" (Tash, 1983:34).

Other channels, such as *suq* (marketplace) gossip and interpersonal communication, also played an important role in spreading the news. This informal, interpersonal communication has maintained an important role among Arabs up to the present (Tash, 1983:35). The mosque still appears to play a major communication role in Yemen, for instance, where Friday prayers are attended by 30 percent of the population.[2] Therefore, the need for more advanced communication tools like newspapers was limited before the nineteenth century (Ayalon, 1995:6). However, two establishments helped introduce the press to the Arab world: colonial powers and the Christian missionaries. The Catholic missionaries in Lebanon, for example, introduced printing as a sign of modernity and civilization. In 1610, Maronite priests brought a printing press equipped with Syriac letters to a Lebanese monastery, and the decades that followed witnessed a competition among the Christian missionaries (Catholic, Greek Orthodox, Protestant) in Lebanon in the use of printing to propagate their beliefs to the masses (Dajani, 1992). Regardless of their aims, their efforts resulted in the spread of literacy, particularly in Lebanon, where several pioneer journalists later helped introduce the profession of journalism in the region. Although several newspapers appeared first in Egypt during the nineteenth century, Lebanon hosted the largest number of newspapers per capita (McFadden, 1953:2). Despite the fact that printing was introduced in the Arab world during the eighteenth century, the first Arab newspaper appeared a century later, which points again to the important role of interpersonal communication. In addition, the printing culture is said to correlate with the establishment of the bourgeoisie, which emerged in the Arab region during the nineteenth century, particularly in Egypt, Lebanon, and Syria (Khodour, 1997:5).

Under the short French rule of Egypt, Napoleon Bonaparte (1798–1800) introduced the first newspaper in the region, albeit in French (Ayalon, 1995:12). The first Arabic newspaper was *Al Tanbeeh*, also during the French rule of Egypt in 1800, according to Abu Bakr (1985:18), although other researchers refer to *Junral Al Iraq*, published in 1816 in Iraq, as the first Arab newspaper (Amin, 2001:24f). Other newspapers were the Arabic-Turkish newspaper, *Waqia al Misriya*, issued in 1828 (Ayalon, 1995; Abu Bakr, 1980), and the Algerian *Al Mubahir*, published in 1847 (Abderrahmane, 1998). More newspapers followed, and some were at the sole initiative of Arab contributors, such as the French and Arabic *Hadikat al-Akhbar* (The Garden of News) in 1870 (Dajani, 1992).

Beginning in the middle of the nineteenth century, the first newspapers in the region were dominated by the Turkish Empire (Essoulami, 2000). In the

Maghrib countries (Morocco, Algeria, and Tunisia), the French colonial power introduced the press as a link between the new colony and the mainland (Kirat, 1987:21; Abderrahmane, 1998). In Egypt, the Turkish ruler Mohamed Ali (1805–1848) patronized the introduction of the press as a means of modernization of the country, and his grandson Ismail (1863–1879) followed in his footsteps in the shrewd utilization of the press in his modernization plans (Ayalon, 1995:16ff).

The content of the early newspapers in the region was limited to official messages from the political establishment regarding internal as well as external affairs. Examining one edition of *Waqia al Misriya* dating back to 1830, for example, Ayalon (1995:17) shows that the items included were randomly mixed and lacked the clear categorization of the news as practiced today. The issue contained accounts of internal matters (the food reserve in the country) and civil trials, as well as accounts of relations with other countries. Political news from other countries was also common, a trend that was widely seen in the early press in other countries as well. (The role of foreign news in the press will be further explored below.)

The first few decades in the history of the Arab press witnessed a modernization of the content as well as the form of newspapers. One major reason for this was the fact that the pioneer journalists, particularly in Lebanon and Syria, were part of the intellectual elite who did not enter journalism to make profit; indeed, journalism was not a source of profit (Abu Zeid, 1993:17). Due to the restrictions imposed by the Turkish authorities and the religious and ethnic conflicts in their countries, Lebanese and Syrian journalists had to flee to elsewhere in the region, as well as to Europe, Russia, and the United States (Abu Zeid, 1993:17). In Egypt, these journalists were regarded as "the intellectual cream of the Near East" by the French ruler Cromer, and they not only dominated the profession but also made it an attractive field for intellectuals (Ayalon, 1995:52). The political stability in their new societies and their encounters with western publications' progressive printing culture allowed the expatriate journalists and other intellectuals to improve the style and content of their publications. The first emigrated Arab newspaper, *Mir'at al Ahwal* (The Mirror of Events), published in 1855 in Turkey, was utilized by its founder Rizqallah Hassoun Al Halabi as a channel to publish his political essays criticizing the policies in the Ottoman Empire, and this led to the closing of the publication within one year of its birth (Abu Zeid, 1993:21). Another publication, *Birjis Baris* (The Paris Jupiter), first published in 1858, was an example of rich content and a modern press style. Political and literary styles were featured in the publication, whose founder was claimed to be one of the pioneers in modernizing the Arab press language by introducing the word for newspaper, *sahifa*, into Arabic (Ayalon, 1995:46f).

Arab intellectuals realized soon enough the power of the press as a political mobilization instrument and a means of disseminating their political and ideological beliefs. In the Maghrib countries, Muslims paid great attention to the role of the press in enhancing their Islamic identity or *shakhsia islamiya* (Abderrahmane, 1998). Rulers also shared this utilitarian view of the press and began patronizing the publications that applauded their politics. For instance, Mohamed Ali's grandson Ismail (1863–1879) bought shares in the French *Le Temps* to guarantee its favorable coverage of his country's affairs and bribed several local papers in Istanbul and patronized local journalists in Egypt (Ayalon, 1995:19).

The press then served political and nationalist purposes in several Arab countries by the end of nineteenth century and the beginning of the twentieth century. Yet, the political beliefs expressed in the press reflected neither the opinions of indigenous intellectuals nor groups of foreign sympathizers. In Algeria, whose press history is rather unique in the Arab world, the colonial press established to serve the authorities was accompanied by the settlers' and "indigenophile" press expressing sympathy for the indigenous people's problems without necessarily questioning the French presence in the country (Kirat, 1987:23f). They called for more rights for the indigenous people and offered them a forum for discussing some minor problems.

Inflamed by their nationalist struggle in the early twentieth century, Arab journalists did not use the press to deliver news (*khabar*) but rather opinion and views (*maqal*). It was also a period of questioning the national identity and the cultural heritage of those intellectuals. That was probably one reason why the press prospered as a forum for political debate in countries like Egypt, Lebanon, Syria, and Algeria, where European colonialism was seen as the greatest threat to sustaining the national identity, while Saudi Arabia and Jordan, which enjoyed political stability and independence, did not develop the same press tradition (Ayalon, 1995:74). Consequently, since its dawn the Arab press has been linked to politics, because it served the settlers' and later the nationalists' aims (McFadden, 1953:1). Also, the high illiteracy rate in the region in the early twentieth century, combined with a lack of adequate advertising revenues, forced the newspapers to depend for their survival on subsidies from various political factions, who in return saw in the press an extended channel to promote their principles (McFadden, 1953:7f). In other countries where there was political stability, the press was a channel for intellectuals to publish their literary productions, focusing less on political content, albeit with a few news items on national events (Tash, 1983:39f). The literary genre also dominated some Egyptian publications that constituted an inspirational source for the development of the press in other countries in the region; the first generation of journalists in those countries were Egyptians (Tash,

1983:39). The literary function of the press was inspired by the European tradition at that time, particularly the French. European journalists regarded themselves as "high literary creators and cosmopolitan political thinkers" (Schudson, 2003:85). The French, for instance, did not bother collecting news and were content with translating the content of British newspapers while they focused on writing their commentaries, where the border between fact and opinion was blurred (Schudson, 2003:85). Rugh (1987:19) argues that professional Arab journalists have always belonged to the well-educated elites who probably could have had careers outside the mass media. That is why, he resumed, the Arab press still contains more regular literature sections compared to western newspapers. Literature serves another function, enforcing the Arab cultural identity, exactly as do the electronic media when they carry Arab music and drama (Rugh, 1987:20).

News as a Unionization Tool

After obtaining their independence, the new national Arab governments saw in the press a potential and a threat: the press's ability to mobilize public opinion, particularly among the elite, versus its power to menace the ideological foundations of governments. Thus, the censorship imposed by law on Arab journalists before independence did not end with the advent of national governments. The French law of 1881 imposed on the Maghrib countries required as a condition for being granted a publication license that the founders not only seek French nationality but also adopt the French language and culture (Abderrahmane, 1998). Several Muslim nationalists were therefore denied access to the media scene. After Algerian independence, the press system was nationalized and turned into a mouthpiece for the government's developmental policies. In Tunisia, the press, although privately owned, showed great loyalty to the government's policies, while in Morocco, the press was seen as more "diverse" and thus enjoyed some autonomy (Abderrahmane, 1998).[3] The first years of independence in several Arab countries witnessed the establishment of new dailies whose main purpose was to promote the new governments' interests. Several of the existing newspapers, however, were forced to stop publishing, either because they lost their political and economic support or because the new laws and regulations hindered their existence.

In Egypt, the party press had to stop publishing after the government dissolved it and confiscated its money in 1953 (Abdel Rahman, 1989:18). The relationship between the Free Officers in Egypt, who led the revolution of 1952 in Egypt, and journalists was rather hostile because the former did not approve of the opinions expressed in the Egyptian press at that time. Censorship was then re-imposed by several acts, the first of which was Military Act 51 in 1953 to "preserve order and ensure security" (Abdel Rahman, 1989:19). That was, according to Abdel Rahman (1989:22), the beginning of detaching the Egyptian press from its main function, informing readers. Nevertheless, the new government did not overlook the important role of the press; Abdel Nasser (1952–1970) supervised the task of appointing new editors-in-chief, a policy followed by his successor Anwar Sadat (1970–1981) (Nasser, 1990). This consequently forced journalists into a vicious circle of self-censorship to ensure that their work would be published. Abdel Nasser himself said at one occasion that there were no restrictive laws on the press and that journalists themselves chose to ignore certain issues out of self-censorship (Nasser, 1979). This circle was broken, however, for a short period in the wake of the 1967 War, when the Arab defeat was said by the press to be the natural outcome of failing Arab policies. The Egyptian government allowed the criticism as "a way of absorbing public resentment" at that time (Abdel Rahman, 1989:33f).

In general, the press was regulated so that it promoted the government's developmental aims by writing about governmental projects and encouraging people to buy locally manufactured goods. As a consequence, the press turned into a mere mouthpiece for national governments. Even in Saudi Arabia, where citizens had a free right to establish publications, the government turned the General Directorate of Broadcasting, Press and Publication into the Ministry of Information and assigned it the task of regulating press ownership. The committee recommended two solutions: limiting government advertising to one main publication (*Um Al Qura*, established in 1924) and compensating the rest of the publications via secret subsidies, or limiting newspaper ownership to organizations, leaving the government the right to license publications and appoint editors-in-chief. The Saudi government chose the second solution, which was adopted in 1963 (Tash, 1983:40f). Newspapers were introduced in Kuwait and Bahrain during the first three decades of the twentieth century.[4] Qatar, the Emirates, and Oman had to wait until the 1970s to establish their own national publications, which gradually increased in number and marked those countries' march into modernization (Moaw'ad, 2000:12ff).

Following its independence in 1943, Lebanon witnessed the emergence of a number of newspapers whose founders saw the press as a business enterprise rather than a cultural project (Dajani, 1992). The media reflected the diversity of Lebanese society, with each newspaper or medium representing a political or religious faction. Nevertheless, Lebanon managed to become the beacon of the Arab region, particularly during the 1950s, when the Egyptian press was nationalized and could no longer fulfill its pan-Arab role. However, the outbreak of the civil war in Lebanon from 1975 until 1990 resulted in the decline of a number of publications, not to mention restrictive press laws imposed in that critical period (Hammoud & Afifi, 1994:162). The conflict among the various political and religious factions in Lebanon made journalists ignore the press laws, and therein lies the main problem of the Lebanese press: "its inability to serve the genuine interests of Lebanese society," instead of indulging in political and religious propaganda for their benefactors (Dajani, 1992:44). The same tendency has been familiar in the Arab world. In 1937, Egypt had 250 publications despite the fact that the illiteracy rate was 86 percent, while the available publications at the moment do not exceed 55, despite an illiteracy rate of 45 percent. Also, in Iraq, there were only around 39 publications under the rule of Saddam Hussein, but Iraqi readers have been bombarded with new publications, now reaching almost 200, since the end of the Iraq war, with each publication representing a political or religious faction in the country (Soloway, 2003). The huge number of publications, combined with low advertising revenues and difficult economic situations in several Arab countries, necessitates dependence on subsidies for survival and pushes journalists to serve the aims of their benefactors in their domestic as well as regional and international coverage (Dajani, 1992).

A country that enjoyed a relatively diverse press despite abiding by its benefactors' rules is Morocco. The Moroccan press can be divided into three categories: pro-government, critical of the government, and anti-government (Abderrahmane, 1998). Amin (2001:25) divides the press system in Morocco into only two main categories: pro-government and oppositional. Apart from the loyal pro-government press, the press is granted some amount of critical freedom "as long as they respect the official line" (Amin, 2001:25). Although the country enjoys a large number of publications, both in Arabic and French, in addition to more than 1,000 publications from France and other Arab and European countries (Abderrahmane, 1998), the government still controls the media.

In general, press ownership in the Arab world following the independence of the Arab states can be divided into three major categories:

1. Private ownership (Saudi Arabia, Kuwait, Lebanon, Tunisia, Morocco, Sudan, Jordan, and the United Arab Emirates)
2. Mixed ownership, that is, private ownership under government control (Egypt, Algeria, and Yemen)
3. Public ownership (Syria, although it now has allowed for conditional forms of private ownership, Libya, and the former Iraqi regime) (Khodour, 1997:13).

Forms of Control

Although private ownership of newspapers is allowed in several Arab countries, Arab governments have reserved the right to grant publishing licenses.

License issuing laws differ from one country to another. In Kuwait, it is the Ministry of Information that holds this right, while in Saudi Arabia and Bahrain, it is in the hands of the Minister of Information. In the United Arab Emirates, this right is granted by a decree from the Ministers Council, and in Lebanon, although it is the Minister of Information who holds the final responsibility, the license is subject to prior acceptance of the National Press Council. This situation is deemed to violate the very essence of freedom of opinion and communication in the Arab world (Al Jammal, 2001:130). As if this were not enough, access to the journalism profession itself is subject to individual countries' policies, despite the fact that the majority of Arab constitutions have not addressed such rules. The authorities justify this interference by the need to maintain political and social stability. The rules address broadcast and print journalists directly, whereas the advertising industry, for example, is not directly affected. While Egypt, Sudan, Saudi Arabia, Lebanon, Tunisia, and Morocco do not limit access to the field, Kuwait, Bahrain, Qatar, Oman, Syria, Yemen, Libya, and Algeria require that journalists obtain a license (Al Jammal, 2001:59ff).

Even after a newspaper founder deals with these issues, there is a larger issue: taboo subjects as defined by ethical charters and national laws. In Algeria, for instance, the Code of Information of 1982 stresses the adherence of journalists to the "objectives of the [Algerian] revolution" defined by the Party of the National Liberation Front (Kirat, 1987:85). Usually, the government may conceal information if it is claimed to endanger state security or reveal economic and military strategies. In Yemen, a new Press and Publication Law was adopted in 1990 to ensure that printed articles are "within the limits of the law."[5] In Egypt, Law 156 of 1960 turned journalists into public servants, and before that, Law 162 of 1958 gave the president the right to declare a state of emergency and thus censor publications and hinder freedom of opinion if it is deemed to collide with national interests. The latter law is still in effect; it was amended in 1980 and 1981, and has been evoked almost continuously since then. The Egyptian government even managed to extend it for another three years by a decree from the People's Assembly (*majlis Al Shaab*) in 2003.[6] Although private ownership was (re)enforced by a law in 1980,[7] the government at the time, under Sadat's rule, enforced the Law of Shame (Law 148), which prohibits the publishing or broadcasting of pictures and texts that may offend the dignity of the state (Nasser, 1990). In Syria, private ownership was legalized in 2001 by Decree 50, but the government has maintained the right to deny licenses "for reasons related to the public interest."[8]

In addition, besides the "risky" topics deemed threatening to the stability of the nation, other issues may also be deemed inappropriate for printing. For example, some Arab states prohibit the printing of crime news because it may spread a feeling of insecurity among the citizens, while other countries allow the printing of such news if the police are portrayed as vigilant and efficient (Al Jammal, 2001:152).

The penalties journalists may face for transgressing these rules vary from administrative to judicial. Saudi Arabia, Qatar, Oman, Syria, Yemen, and Libya provide the administrative authorities with the freedom to confiscate publications or prohibit their distribution in cases where they assess newspaper policy to be in conflict with state policy or to serve the interests of foreign regimes. Egypt, Sudan, and Lebanon apply judicial penalties in such cases, while Bahrain, the Emirates, Tunisia, Algeria, and Morocco combine administrative and judicial penalties (Al Jammal, 2001:62).

The control exercised over newspapers has also been applied to the electronic media: radio and television. In fact, radio and television broadcasting are the states' absolute monopolies for three main reasons. First, broadcasting is given more priority than the printing press because of its ability to reach all citizens, regardless of their education, thus illiteracy—a filter to access to print culture—does not prevent access to radio and television programs, usually made in local vernaculars. Second, these media play a major role in sustaining national unity and spreading the feeling of community among citizens. Third, electronic media may serve as a main instrument in the political propaganda machine, which would be dangerous in hostile hands (Amin, 2001:29). Development of the television system was even initiated by the states' considerations of these same factors.[9] The Saudi government, for instance, appeared to establish television broadcasting to distract citizens from foreign programs—and provide them with a sense of community—and to serve the kingdom's developmental projects by means of educational programs (Tash, 1983:51). Another reason for establishing electronic media, particularly television, is that they are symbols of the national modernization process. El-Sherif (1980:28) points to the ability of some small emirates in the Gulf to live without an army as long as they can afford their daily newspapers and their radio and television as signs of economic prosperity and integration in the modern world. Amin (2001:29) divides Arab broadcasting systems into two main types: those that adhere to a national, mobilization unity (Algeria, Libya, Egypt, Iraq, Syria, Yemen, and the Sudan) and those that adhere to a bureaucratic, laissez-faire philosophy, comprising the rest of the Arab states except Lebanon and Morocco, who have control over broadcast media but do not exercise this right as rigidly as the first group.

The oral culture of the region is said to be the reason why radio plays an important role as a mass medium, especially when the illiteracy rate is still high. Some Arab politicians have paid great attention to the use of radio, and subsequently television, as a channel to disseminate their political beliefs not only within the borders of their countries but also to other Arab peoples in the region. One example was Egyptian President Gamal Abdel Nasser (1952–1970) who used the radio as a primary means to strengthen his position in Egypt and the Arab world in general (Ghareeb, 2000). During the 1960s and 1970s, Arab radio stations were the main weapons used in factional struggles, which made the slogan "radio in the service of development" lose its meaning (Khodour, 1997:19f). The same slogan accompanied the establishment of television broadcasting in several Arab countries, yet soon enough the new medium turned into just another mobilization tool on the Arab political scene. In fact, Khodour (1997:22f) argues that the establishment of television broadcasting was the result of political decrees with no preparation, whether in terms of technical equipment or manpower, which had to come from the press and radio.

Laws and regulations are not the only means of controlling the press; control also comes from within, namely the journalists' self-control. In the Palestinian areas, journalists avoid certain issues due to their belief that their profession is a "patriotic mission" (Al Khatib, 2002:12). In Algeria, journalists are used to avoiding complex issues that may provoke the authorities, even if the readers would like to read more about such issues (Kirat, 1987:199). Turkistani's study (1989:249) among media institutions in four Arab countries confirmed this tendency to self-censor, which is maintained through self-control and acknowledgement of the limits of how news gets covered and presented. Many, if not all, editors prefer to play it safe and not cover controversial items. The editor-in-chief gives instructions as to what to avoid and what to cover based on the government's position. The editor-in-chief of *Al Hayat*, Jihad Khazen, admits that the most prevalent censorship now is self-censorship. The main concern for his daily, for instance, is not to stir any national conflicts in Saudi Arabia, where the newspaper cannot afford to be banned, or else they "stand to lose tens of thousands of dollars in advertising revenue." In Sudan, where the currency is worthless, banning the newspaper does not constitute such a financial threat (Khazen, 1999).

The concept of news as "public knowledge" was first introduced by the colonial authorities with the main aim of informing officials in their local administration of laws and regulations imposed from abroad. The goal was therefore mainly instructive. Then, indigenous people, particularly the intellectuals, saw in the press a new form of communication, mainly as a new channel for their intellectual debates and literary productions. In the first half of the twentieth century, prior to the independence of several Arab states, the indigenous nationalists used the press as a forum to discuss their independence, a role that was deemed significant for mobilizing public opinion against the imperialist powers. Because of that very role, newly independent governments realized that the press was a powerful weapon and they sought to monopolize it. Although the time was ripe for the press to take up the internal affairs issues that were marginalized, giving place to anti-imperialist opinions, that did not happen. National governments wanted to use the news media as a vehicle to promote their national development policies and to mobilize pan-Arab public opinion. Nasser, for instance, used the Egyptian radio *Sawt Al Arab* (Voice of the Arabs) to mobilize public opinion. Even popular cultural genres have been utilized in the mobilization battle. Egyptian radio stations have followed a new strategy since the beginning of the recent Iraq war: they send songs calling for Arab nationalism, peace, and support for the Palestinian *Intifada*. Modern love songs disappeared from the programs and were replaced by religious and national songs (*Al Sharq Al Awsat*, 2 April 2003).

Poverty and the high illiteracy rates in the region did not contribute to the commercialization of media for the benefit of a new bourgeoisie, as was the case in the United States. Although the current changes on the Arab media scene suggest the emergence of commercialized media, Arab audiences still get huge doses of political debate and news concerning pan-Arab issues and foreign affairs but little on their internal social problems. This is because the new channels, particularly satellite channels, like the large-circulation, pan-Arab-marketed newspapers, simply have to rely on foreign relations issues to attract audiences from all over the region. This is even manifested in the use of language: such media outlets use Modern Standard Arabic (MSA) rather than the vernaculars in their debates, thus marking their pan-Arab character (the issue of the use of MSA will be discussed in detail in chapters six and seven).

As long as foreign affairs remain the driving force behind political debates, no channel will focus on local issues. Also, political culture plays an important role in fostering this attitude: public opinion has practically no influence on governmental policies, and the news media—no matter how democratized—can never be a substitute for genuine political institutions that involve the public. In other words, Arab citizens have no power to exercise. For instance, ballots and opinion polls play no significant role in forming national or regional policies. Perhaps this is why tabloids (or the yellow press as Arab commentators prefer to call them) have attracted audiences by focusing on local affairs. (The tabloidization of the press will be discussed further in chapter four.)

Establishing news media outlets alone could not have served the intentions of Arab regimes, unless they also controlled the information flow to these media. Thus, each state built a national news agency serving as a bureaucratic gatekeeper to liaise between foreign news sources and local news media.

News Agencies: The Bureaucratic Gatekeeper

The history of Arab news agencies dates back to 1956, when the Egyptian news agency, Middle East News Agency (MENA), was established to serve the whole region (Abu Bakr, 1985). However, some researchers claim that the Sudanese News Agency was established in 1945 and thus is actually the oldest in the region (Al Jammal, 2001; Khalil, 1983). Moreover, the year 1959 witnessed the birth of four news agencies: the Iraqi News Agency, Tunis Afrique Press, Maghrib Arab Press (Morocco), and the Lebanese National News Agency.[10] The Algerian news agency, Algerie Presse Service, followed in 1961, then the Jordanian and the Syrian news agencies in 1964 and 1965, respectively. The 1970s witnessed the establishment of the Gulf news agencies (Saudi Arabia, Qatar, Kuwait, and United Arab Emirates) besides the Yemeni and Palestinian agencies.[11]

Yet the role of the Arab news agencies was limited (Khalil, 1983:126) by a lack of the financial, technical, and human resources of the well-established western news agencies. The special cultural bond among Gulf countries contributed to the establishment of several sub-regional projects, among them Gulfvision and the Gulf News Agency (Abdel Rahman, 1989:54). Thanks to the prosperity of petrol wealth, the regional agencies have sophisticated technology (Harris & Malczek, 1979:6). Common among all agencies is that they are government-controlled (Al Jammal, 2001), and the employees are therefore regarded as public servants. The correspondents of the Syrian news agency were even regarded as diplomats (Abu Bakr, 1985:23).

Prior to the First World War, the news flow to and from the Arab region was controlled by the British and French agencies. In 1866, Reuters established its regional office in Alexandria, Egypt (Ayalon, 1995:19), and dominated the British colonized territories, while the French established local offices in the Maghrib countries and later in Syria and Lebanon (Rugh, 1987:134f). This monopoly was broken after the Second World War by the American Associated Press (AP) and United Press International (UPI), who, according to Rugh (1987:135), were sought out by Arab media to meet the increasing demand of their audience for foreign news and to break free of the European monopoly. Although the Arab peoples' interest in international news could have increased tremendously after the Second World War and their independence, there is some evidence that this interest in foreign news began long before.[12] In addition, the position of Agènce France Presse (AFP) and Reuters was ensured in the region even after independence. AFP offered its service in French to the North African markets in Algeria, Tunisia, and Morocco, as well as to Lebanon. In an attempt to compete with the French, Reuters offered a French translation of its bulletin, to which the French replied by offering an English translation of its bulletin (Rugh, 1987:137). The dominant position of both the British and the French (and to some extent the American) press agencies made some Arab researchers warn against the flood of foreign cultural products into the region, especially with the local agencies busy in their own conflicts with the Arab regimes (Abdel Rahman, 2002). One Egyptian media researcher concluded his study on the sociology of news in the Egyptian press by recommending the establishment of an interdisciplinary committee to handle the incoming news from western agencies and pass on what it thought was suitable, since ordinary reporters were not thought capable of handling the subtlety of this news by themselves (Abdel Nabi, 1989). The position of the European agencies (Reuters and AFP) was further strengthened by the introduction of the Arabic version of their news bulletin in the 1960s (Rugh, 1987:137). Although later in the 1970s this dominant position was challenged by the wide variety of sources available to Arab editors from other countries, Arab media still favored the American, British, and French sources (Rugh, 1987:139).

The main function of the local Arab news agencies was to assist the government in disseminating its information and controlling the incoming news from foreign sources (Khalil, 1983; Rugh, 1987). The news dominated by local agencies is primarily national; some agencies even monopolize it, and some serve as the main source of foreign news, which is subjected to re-editing according to the country's media policy (Al Jammal, 2001:90). The Libyan news agency, for instance, not only monopolizes the local news, but also serves as a gatekeeper and sole distributor of incoming foreign news (Amin, 2001:26). In some countries, the local news agencies are the sole organs permitted to subscribe to foreign news sources (Rugh, 1987:143f), with the objective of preventing negative news about the local government from spreading. As a Tunisian official, quoted in Rugh (1987:144), put it: "We guard against lies about Tunisia and take care to avoid disturbing public opinion." In Saudi Arabia, Qatar, Kuwait, and Morocco, the local media are permitted to obtain foreign news directly from international sources (Rugh, 1987:135f).

The dominance of local news agencies is seen as the main reason for the monotony of the news published in most dailies. For instance, a Saudi journalist mocked the Saudi dailies' quoting the hard news distributed by the Saudi news agency as if it were "a sacred text," whereas the only variation comes with the coverage of sports or entertainment (Koeppel, 1989:3). In spite of the sophisticated equipment in some agencies, particularly in the Gulf countries, they seem to suffer technical problems that hinder efficient news exchange with foreign agencies (Abdel Rahman, 2002:91). Until 1983, some local agencies did not even keep statistics or records on their news exchanges (Khalil, 1983:127). Another problem facing several of the local agencies is the lack of adequate training for their personnel (Khalil, 1983; Abu Bakr, 1985). Khalil (1983) visited seven of the local agencies and interviewed officials there on personnel performance. Only two of them regarded their manpower as satisfactory (Khalil, 1983:127). This issue, combined with the lack of modern technology and the limited exchange activities among Arab countries, were seen as the main problems facing them (Abu Bakr, 1985:24f).

Despite the factors that bind the Arab countries—common (written) language, common interest and strategies (Al Jammal, 2001:91)—the news exchange among them is limited to only 2 percent (Abdel Rahman 2002). Turkistani (1989) found that in the four countries included in his study (Saudi Arabia, Tunisia, Algeria, and Kuwait), there was little "Arab" news that was mainly provided by local agencies through the Arabsat exchange (Turkistani,1989:238). The conservative attitude in some countries, particularly in the Gulf, is one reason behind the limited exchange in the region (Turkistani,1989:267). This conservatism has led some Lebanese newspapers and magazines to print different editions, with the conservative versions confined to the Gulf region. For example, the Lebanese magazine *Ash-Shabaka* had to print two different editions of its issue on March 18, 1973, with one edition featuring a girl in a bikini and another edition (mainly distributed in Saudi Arabia and Libya) with the only the face of the girl (Dajani, 1992). Another reason is that bilateral relations with other countries determine the flow of news to and from (and probably also about) these countries (Khalil, 1983:137). In general, a lack of coordination among Arab officials responsible for the media, bureaucracy, and the different needs of each country are among the main reasons for the limited news exchange in the region (Turkistani, 1989:256). For Abdel Rahman (2002), the Arab agencies are too busy with propaganda for their own regimes to properly coordinate the news exchange among themselves, thus allowing the western agencies to play the crucial role in news dissemination.

Some Arab agencies look up to the long experience of the western news agencies and regard this as one of the main differences between Arab and western agencies and also the reason behind the latter's dominant role (Turkistani, 1989:255f). Other reasons are the high technical quality of news flowing from the West. This news is also characterized as being more objective and providing background information lacking in the Arab news (Turkistani, 1989:255f). This results in an "unbalanced flow of information" between West and East, exemplified by the western agencies' disinterest in the developing countries juxtaposed with the admiration of the Arab agencies for their western counterparts (Khalil, 1983:140f). This means the flow of news in one direction, West to East. A previous study from 1976 on the news flow between Eurovision and the Egyptian television system showed that Eurovision showed only one item from Egypt, the only item sent. Egyptian television, on the other hand, showed fifteen out of the 161 items sent by Eurovision (Rugh, 1987:146). This despite the fact that news from the Middle East is still prioritized by the European agencies (Hjarvard, 1995a:206). Turkistani (1989:238) found that the local news is covered by local news agencies, while Arab news, if any, is obtained either via exchange agreements with other Arab countries or though the international news exchange. He also found that the amount of Arab news in television newscasts is rather limited.

International news agencies play an important role in providing international news, both pictures and scripts, and the French AFP is used more extensively in the former French colonies of Algeria and Tunisia (Turkistani, 1989:238). In one study on the coverage of the 1991 Gulf War in Egyptian newspapers, Abdel Rahman (2002) shows that international news agencies were the main providers of news to Arab media, even news coming from Iraq or other Arab countries, and even in the Egyptian newspaper *Al Ahram*, which has several correspondents and offices abroad. Another finding was the abundance of unidentified sources in the news items. As these items do not carry a byline, it is difficult to identify their sources.

Local news agencies, moreover, are exposed to financial and political pressure from the local regimes. Economically, state organs can favor their loyal publications with advertising contracts, cutting off those who have not shown the same loyalty (Koeppel, 1989). The political pressure exerted on news sources varies according to the regime's policy, but generally Arab news agencies work on acclaiming "the achievements of the many sectors of the state" (Amin, 2001:25). Even foreign news organizations, however, are not exempt from state control. According to Koeppel (1989:12), the Syrian government, for example, did not allow foreign news agencies to establish permanent offices in the country, and it confined the task of newsgathering to local journalists. Foreign correspondents' residence permits in the region may be shortened and they may face expulsion or denial of visas if their work offends the authorities (Koeppel, 1989:12f). Even local journalists who work for foreign agencies are not regarded as the real representatives of these agencies; their role is confined to stringers with no direct contact with the main offices in Europe (or the United States) but only with the agencies' "real" correspondents in the region, usually stationed in Cairo, Cyprus, or Beirut (Al Imam, 2002). The role of foreign agencies seems therefore to be gathering the news through their hired correspondents (or gatekeepers) in the region and then reselecting and editing it to fit the policy of the media institution (Al Imam, 2002).

In fact, foreign news reporting has received the attention of several Arab scholars due to the general dependency of Arab media on international news agencies as news sources. They see these sources as western-oriented, fulfilling a sort of mobilization function for their governments, although this argument can now be applied only to the print press, due to the limited financial resources available for it to hire its own correspondents. Arab editors acknowledge that they choose to concentrate on foreign news rather than local news because local news is boring protocol news (Turkistani, 1989:251f). In addition, the media seem to exercise an agenda-setting function only with regard to foreign affairs (Schudson, 2003:160; Al Haqeel & Melkote, 1995:34).

Foreign News

Since the early days of the press, foreign news has served as an indicator of its modernization, and perhaps of that of the whole society. During the colonial period, American editors were content to fill their papers with news from elsewhere, and readers were hungry for more news from Europe, particularly during periods of military activity (Cassara, 2002:248). Then, foreign news was a competitiveness factor for the penny press, and correspondents were sent to Europe to write on the major events there and send it in letters to the newspapers, thus the name "foreign correspondence" (Cassara, 2002:248). Neither editors nor readers showed much interest in local events, which were known by everybody. In addition, it was "safer" to write on foreign news than on local events to escape governmental censorship (Green, 2002:37). In Egypt, too, foreign news was compiled and translated from the *Times, World, L'Independence Belge*, Reuters, and other sources (Haeri, 2003:74). In fact, the Arab journalist Ibrahim Al Yaziji (1847–1906)[13] criticized the amount of foreign news in the Egyptian press at the end of the nineteenth century. He could not fathom why the press reported on European politics or wars between Japan and China, "or all these events that did not interest the Egyptians" (Abboud, 1984:16). Nevertheless, the development of the Arab press was marked by an increasing amount of foreign news, not only provided by or translated from foreign sources, but also provided by the newspapers' own correspondents, whose knowledge of other cultures fascinated their readers.

Recalling the heyday of his job as the first Egyptian correspondent abroad, Mohamed H. Heikal, who later became the editor-in-chief of *Al Ahram*, wrote, "Everybody was fascinated by my foreign experience and my knowledge of coups d'etat." He was one of the country's celebrities, and the sensational headlines accompanying his accounts used to announce the young correspondent's adventures: "Heikal enters Korea"; "Heikal writes from Iran."[14] He admitted that covering foreign news, no matter how risky, was nevertheless far more prestigious and beneficial to his career than reporting on local political affairs "behind closed doors." His accounts, not only legendary and captivating for his audience, later earned him a prestigious governmental post.

For both readers and journalists, foreign news reporting is an exciting showground. Foreign news is normally seen to aim at a certain segment of the audience: the well-educated, well-informed, and knowledgeable (Holm et al.,

2000:22). For journalists, it is also a privilege to work with the whole world as a basis, rather than with local news (Holm et al., 2000:37). Foreign news is not only a sign of modernity and openness of the nation, but it is also the place where the images of "us" and "them" are clearly manifested.

The 1970s and 1980s brought worldwide interest in international news coverage. This followed complaints by several developing countries that they were misrepresented in the industrial world's media. To discuss that matter, UNESCO arranged a global debate under the title "The New World Information and Communication Order." The debate resulted in several studies on international news coverage, among them Sreberny-Mohammadi et al. (1985) and Stevenson & Shaw (1986). The debate revolved around the claim that the news media of the developed countries neglected the poor countries and preferred to assign their correspondents to a few rich capitals. Even when the poor countries made it to the front pages, it was almost always in connection with a disaster or violent acts, thus bolstering the customary stereotypes of these countries as regions of disturbance.

Even prior to that debate, international news coverage in the Arab press concerned media scholars, as the Arab press was seen to pay disproportional attention to western events, perhaps due to the European occupation of the major part of the region. Abu-lughod (1962) sought in his study of international news in seven Arab dailies to determine the amount and kind of international news to which Arab readers were exposed and the overall attitudes toward the foreign countries mentioned in the news. He noticed extensive coverage of the United States, Britain, the USSR, and France. A positive attitude was shown in coverage of the USSR, then the United States, while the coverage of both Britain and France was largely negative. The amount of foreign news was not equally represented in all Arab newspapers examined. In fact, the Saudi press showed a tendency to focus on local news rather than international news, which in all occupied only 9 percent of the total news space (Abu-lughod, 1962:603). This tendency in the Saudi press (and the Gulf press in general) was further confirmed in later studies (Harris & Malczek, 1979; Dajani, 1989). Although their focus was on how other countries were represented in the Arab press, Arab journalists also researched how other presses presented the Arab region. A survey among Algerian journalists showed that they regard news as a means to "counterattack foreign propaganda" and to provide factual information (Kirat, 1987:169f).

In the Arab region, Arab (or pan-Arab) news has been prioritized in the Arab press, probably at the expense of foreign news where no Arab actors are involved. One content analysis of *Al Hayat* showed that Arab news occupied 68 percent, while foreign news occupied 32 percent (Abu Zeid, 1993:392f).

The same newspaper depends on its correspondents (43 percent) and its London office (22 percent) rather than international news agencies (9 percent) (Abu Zeid, 1993:392f). Another analysis of several Arab newspapers confirms the priority given to Arab news (Al Jammal, 1990). One content analysis of foreign news in two Jordanian newspapers pointed to the priority given to foreign news involving Arabs, thus contributing to the increase in Third World news. Still, politics is by far the dominant issue in foreign news (Al Jammal, 1990; Abu Zeid, 1993; Rachty, 1978; Abu-lughod, 1962; Abdelaziz, 1981; El Sarayrah, 1986; Dajani, 1989). Moreover, Palestinian dailies have shifted away from covering domestic affairs to focusing on the foreign policy of the Palestinian Authority (Jamal, 2001:275f).

On the other hand, recent surveys among American audiences have shown that they do not feel well informed about the current world situation and therefore seek more foreign news coverage. Nevertheless, and despite the fact that the American news media are commercialized and subject to the audiences' needs, the amount of international news is in constant decline in the American news media, which gives more and more space to local news.[15] This is rather paradoxical, considering the hegemony of the United States as the only superpower. However, the American news media's inclination to prioritize local news, assuming that this is what the audience demands, seems to echo the situation in other countries.

The amount of foreign news in the Arab media is in fact higher than that in the American media. One content analysis of foreign news in four American newspapers and five Arab newspapers showed that the latter devoted more than 30 percent of their news space to international news, while the American newspapers devoted only 11 percent (Abdelaziz, 1981). It is interesting that in both media the other party ranked second in the list of countries or regions mentioned most frequently in the news; thus, the United States occupied the second largest space in Arab foreign news, and likewise the Arab region occupied the second largest space in the American newspapers. In both cases, Europe held the first place in foreign news reporting (Abdelaziz, 1981). Contrary to the developing countries' complaints in the 1970s and 1980s about the decreased coverage of their news, Arab scholars point at the increasing amount of news from the developing world, including the Arab news (Al Jammal, 1990; El Sarayrah, 1986). It can be argued, however, that the amount of news about a certain region is not only a matter of priority of the region's news but rather a question of availability of such news from news suppliers, such as news agencies.

The role of news agencies, particularly the big four,[16] has been seen as the most important and consistent factor in the analysis of foreign news coverage (Rachty, 1978; Dajani, 1989; Al Jammal, 1990). While some scholars look distrustfully on the role of international news agencies as the major source of news (Rachty, 1978; Abdel Rahman, 1989; Al Jammal, 1990), others interpret the increasing dependence on these sources as an indicator of openness in the dependent country (Dajani, 1989).

Foreign news provided by the international news agencies about the Arab region is estimated to include factors of "foreign propaganda" and not just sheer news. In his set of recommendations to the Egyptian press, Abdel Nabi (1989) warns Egyptian journalists of the great responsibility in dealing with the news supplied by international (western) news agencies, a matter that requires more qualifications and experience. He therefore suggests the establishment of an interdisciplinary committee to deal with this type of news, rather than leaving this job to novice journalists who cannot grasp the intricacies behind the huge supply of information. This is perhaps why the editor-in-chief of *Al Hayat* boasted about his newspaper's dependence on their own correspondents to cover international events, particularly the 1991 Gulf War, rather than depending on ready-made news packages provided by the big four (Abu Zeid, 1993:392ff).[17]

Stevenson and Shaw (1986:56ff) argue that international news agencies are not as influential as the national news agencies and local journalists (gatekeepers). They conducted content analyses of news in several developing countries and argued that the differences in foreign news covered in each country called for a redefinition of news as politics. They also point to the vast amount of information provided by western agencies, which far exceeded the amount of information used by developing nations' agencies. The vast amount of information then presumes a selection of the type of news as well as the perspectives adopted in narrating it.

The establishment of a joint Arab news agency to balance the dominance of foreign agencies is an idea that has been current but unacted on for forty years. Arab governments, who control the media institutions either directly or indirectly, seem to disagree on both form and content of such a news agency (Qallab, 2002).[18] They disagree on the form it should take, as some countries want the leadership and number of employees to be proportional to population, whereas others think financial resources should be the criterion. They also disagree on the content of the news to be distributed: some countries want to target media propaganda against the United States and the West, seeing the conflict between Arabs and Israel as a conflict with western powers as well. Others prefer to direct propaganda against the danger of communism, which undermines the authority of religion. The lack of one unified Arab foreign policy is regarded as one obstacle to this cooperation (Qallab, 2002). Rugh (1987:148f) listed the following reasons for the failure to establish a joint Arab news agency:

1. Lack of the prerequisite, commercially oriented media found in the West.
2. Lack of a centralized media system due to differing policies among Arab countries.
3. Lack of financial resources (though some wealthy countries could finance such a project alone).
4. Ideological conflicts between countries.

Joint media and communications ventures among Arab countries have proven less than fruitful. For instance, the common satellite ARABSAT[19] did not fulfill its mission of enhancing inter-Arab exchanges or contributing to the development process (Guaaybess, 2002).

It was hoped that the Egyptian bureau MENA would play a major role in the region, but it has been limited by its attachment to the Egyptian government and its policies (Al Imam, 2002). As a result, Egyptian journalists may in fact know little about the events in other Arab countries.[20] Thus, the source of news about the region has been taken over by the international news agencies (particularly the "big four"): AFP distributing news about Lebanon, Reuters distributing news about Morocco, and AP distributing news about Egypt. However, the explosion of TV-satellite channels and their well-established network of correspondents in western countries is redressing the imbalance (Al Imam, 2002).

Another reason for the imbalance is the lack of interest of Arab journalists in reporting on routine news, particularly given the absence of investigative reporting. Instead, novice journalists seek to establish their names as columnists and thereby ensure their fame in the profession (Fandy, 2003). Thus, the task of distributing the news among the newspaper's sections proves simple: news from Reuters goes to the news page, news from AFP to the investigation section , and news from the *New York Times* to the analysis section (Fandy, 2003). As for the content, priority is usually given to political news, followed by economic news. Cultural and human-interest news is usually not in demand among Arab news agencies (Khalil, 1983). Likewise, development news from the region is not of interest to all countries (Turkistani, 1989:254). The news offered by the international agencies, with its high technical quality, background information, newscast length, and objective formulation, are the reasons why Arab news sources still depend on international agencies (Rugh, 1987; Turkistani, 1989).

Arab news agencies fail to provide a rich source of Arab news to Arab media and thereby reduce their dependence on foreign (western) news sources. The agencies' preoccupation with serving the existing regimes or covering routine, local news that is hardly an exchange item for other Arab news agencies is among the reasons for this failure. Another reason, however, is the lack of careful pre-planning common to the whole media sector in the region. The establishment of these agencies was not preceded by careful strategic planning on the part of the founders (governments) regarding the goals and means for achieving them; rather they were regarded as a sheer indicator of Arabs' efforts to modernize their countries (Khodour, 1997:16). The same can be said about the initiation of television broadcasting (El-Sherif, 1980), and it can be argued that the same problem prevailed in academic institutions for journalism. In Algeria, for instance, journalism programs, established in 1964, focus on preparing the students for work in print media, while the country lacks a qualified workforce for the broadcasting sector (Kirat, 1987:76). The establishment of communications departments in Arab countries took place arbitrarily, without addressing serious consequences or even motivation, such as the lack of trained labor and the needs of each country (Al Jammal, 2001:213). The increase in the number of these departments and consequently the number of graduates has meant that not all of them are guaranteed a suitable job in the communications industry. In fact, students are more inclined to major in subjects other than journalism, partially because they want to guarantee suitable jobs in public service and partially because of their fear of getting into conflict with governmental authorities that control the press, directly or indirectly (Al Jammal, 2001:213).

Notes

1. Benson's (2001) study, for instance, has shown that the state-dominated French news media were as critical to the government as American news media. This is perhaps due to these media's need to show their political independence.

2. See the report of the Stanhope Centre for Communications Policy Research on Yemeni press laws. Available online at: www.internews.org/arab_media_research (12 March 2004).

3. The classification of the Arab press as mobilizing, loyalist, and diverse was originally a typology suggested by William Rugh (1987; 2004). See a more detailed discussion of this typology and its criticism in chapter three.

4. The first publication in Kuwait appeared in 1928 and in Bahrain in 1939. Yet, it was not until the 1960s that those countries developed a more sophisticated printing culture in terms of both content and form. Kuwait also witnessed the establishment of a number of magazines, which marked qualitative progress in Kuwaiti media. Among these magazines is *Al Arabi*, established by the Kuwaiti Ministry of Information in 1958, probably the most widely read magazine in the Arab world, with a monthly circulation of 360,000 (figures from 1993). The magazine had to stop publication following the 1991 Gulf War, but resumed publication on 1 September 1991 (Kazan, 1994:148).

5. See the Stanhope Centre for Communications Policy Research, "Study of Media Laws and Politics for the Middle East and Maghrib." Available online at: www.internews.org/arab_media_research.

6. See the Stanhope Centre for Communications Policy Research.

7. Private ownership was allowed before the coup d'état in 1952, when the Free Officers claimed power in Egypt and nationalized the press; private and party-owned press were then prohibited.

8. See the Stanhope Centre for Communications Policy Research on Syrian press laws.

9. Radio broadcasting began first in Algeria in 1925 and in Egypt in 1926, before it spread to other states. Television broadcasting was initiated in Morocco in 1954, and two years later in Algeria, Iraq, and Lebanon before it reached other Arab countries in the 1960s and 1970s (Amin, 2001:29f).

10. Dajani (1992) states that in Lebanon there are around twenty-eight licensed local news agencies and ten registered offices of regional and international news agencies.

11. According to Abu Bakr (1985), the Sudanese National News Agency was also established in 1973.

12. For instance, the Arab journalist Ibrahim Al Yaziji (1847–1906) complained that foreign news in the Egyptian press occupied so much space and doubted that such news was of any interest to Egyptian readers (Abboud, 1984).

13. Al Yaziji (1847–1906) was a Lebanese-born journalist and translator. He moved to Egypt, where he published three journals.

14. Quoted in Nasser (1979:32f).

15. From the report "Bringing the World Home," 1999, American Society of Newspaper Editors. According to another study quoted in this report, only 47 percent of Americans could name Boris Yeltsin as the president of Russia. Other studies quoted confirm the concern of Americans about the lack of coverage of international news, such as the survey conducted by the Freedom Forum's Newseum.

16. The studies cited here refer to the "big four": AP, Reuters, AFP and UPI. However, UPI does not seem to play that important a role any longer, since its output has significantly decreased.

17. In his content analysis of the news in *Al Hayat* in a selected period in 1990, Abu Zeid (1993) pointed at the important role played by the newspaper's correspondents, providing 43 percent of international coverage, followed by the London office, which supplied 22 percent, and the news agencies, which accounted for only 9 percent.

18. Salah Al Qallab, former Jordanian Minister of Information, Commentary, *Al Sharq Al Awsat*, 27 June 2002.

19. ARABSAT was launched in 1976, but it took it one decade to begin operating in space. By 1997, two more satellites were added to the ARABSAT, namely ARABSAT 1-C and 2-A (Ayish, 2001:117).

20. In his commentary in *Al Sharq Al Awsat* on 21 May 2002, Ghassan Al Imam regarded Egyptian journalists' knowledge of other Arab countries to be as slight as their knowledge of Taiwan or Nepal.

3

Categorization of the Arab Press: Rugh's Typology Revisited

News is everywhere democratic only in the sense of being nonexclusive, published information potentially available to anyone who wishes to attend to it. It does not necessarily promote active, empowered citizenship.

—Michael Schudson, *The Sociology of News*

A S A CULTURAL PRODUCT, news is a reflection of its society and the professional standards fostered by journalistic organizations in that society. Accordingly, there is no unified, global categorization of the press but rather a number of categorizations that attempt to account for all cultural differences. One attempt was the classification of the press according to the relationship of media and society. According to this theory, there are four models of the press: authoritarian, libertarian, communist, and social responsibility (Golding & Elliott, 1979; McQuail, 2002). The authoritarian system refers to repressive measures to control the press and prohibit the spread of opinions that might prove threatening to the regime's ideologies. The libertarian system is rooted in the classical writings of Locke and Mill, propagating a new kind of democratic society where private ownership of the press is allowed and ideas and opinions are exchanged freely. The communist system refers to the communist regimes, particularly in the former Soviet Union, where the media were regarded as another tool for the regime to circulate its ideology to the masses. Naturally, public monopoly of media rather than private ownership was the only form allowed under these regimes. The social responsibility theory refers to the system where media show a greater concern for raising the quality of its content, serving all tastes, and representing a full range of opinions. This system is related to the public service broadcasting systems in several Western European countries.

Raymond Williams (Golding & Elliott, 1979:46) proposed a new categorization of four systems based on organizational form rather than political ideologies: the authoritarian; the paternal, which is "an authoritarian system with a conscience," imposing heavy censorship on the media to disseminate only the values deemed advantageous for the masses; the commercial system and the democratic system. Another categorization, the development theory, was suggested by a number of scholars (see McQuail, 2002:155ff, for a fuller discussion), referring to countries in transition from colonialism to independence, where the foundation for freeing and commercializing the media sector has not yet been cultivated.

Arab scholars prefer to describe Arab media systems in terms of either the social responsibility or development theory. Hamada (1993:172) regards the social responsibility theory as the most realistic to apply to the Arab region. This is because media in the developing world should serve the development and political stability needed for these societies, but this does not necessarily mean that the government should maintain a monopoly on the news media. In fact, private ownership should also be allowed, given that the media organizations, public or private, should adhere to the ethical and legislative codes of the country. According to this system, the news media will serve a twofold purpose: first, it will provide sufficient information to promote citizen participation in the political process, and second, it will hold the government accountable for its policies in a watchdog role. Abu Zeid (2000:35ff) adopts the development theory to describe the ideal media system for the Arab region. According to that system, news serves a decisive role in the development of society, while ensuring citizens' full participation in development plans. Accuracy and objectivity are prerequisites for this role, which the news media should fulfill not out of ideological or authoritarian constraints but out of a need to live up to their professional duty to serve society. Abdel Rahman (1983, in Hamada, 1993:169f) proposed a third category that she named "dependency theory." This theory is rooted in the Egyptian economist Samir Amin's explanation of the economic backwardness of the Arab region, according to which the Arab media systems are the result of centuries of colonialism and suppression, and, as such, are dependent on the international news media as sources and inspiration for fostering new journalistic practices.

In light of western theories of the press, William Rugh (2004) proposed the categorization of the Arab press into four systems: mobilization, loyal, diverse, and transitional. Rugh's typology, one of the few comprehensive studies of the

Arab press available, has been very influential in describing Arab media systems. Nonetheless, the typology has its shortcomings. It has been criticized by a number of Arab scholars for being based on unclearly defined categories. Another shortcoming is that the typology, even in its updated version, still does not account for the recent situation in the Arab news media, which has been under rapid development since the 1990s.

The aim of this chapter is to give space to this criticism, illustrating the shortcomings of Rugh's theory and its negligence of several factors, such as the role of émigré newspapers. It begins with a brief review of the typology before examining its criticism in light of previous research on Arab media. Three important factors will be added to the discussion: 1) the relationship between public opinion and the press; 2) the role of Arab newspapers abroad; and 3) Rugh's implied bias against Arab journalism, particularly when compared to American journalism.

Evaluation of the Typology

In his analysis of the Arab press, Rugh categorizes the Arab press into four types:

1. Mobilized press in Syria, Libya, and the Sudan, where national governments use the media as a political mobilization tool. Common among these countries is that they were under European colonialism and have developed their media systems in times of political instability.
2. Loyalist press in Saudi Arabia, Oman, Palestine, Bahrain, Qatar, and the United Arab Emirates. Here, an amount of freedom is granted to the press and private ownership is allowed. However, indirect control is still exercised by the national governments, and the press owners themselves exhibit great loyalty to the existing regimes and their ideologies.
3. Diverse press in Kuwait, Morocco, Yemen, Iraq, and Lebanon, characterized by less authoritarianism and a diversity of opinion.
4. Transitional press systems in Algeria, Egypt, Jordan, and Tunisia, of which, according to Rugh, it "is not clear which way they are headed or indeed that they are in fact in transition to a different type of system that will stabilize and remain for a long time" (2004:134).

Rugh (2004:253) tabularizes this typology as illustrated in the following table.

Table 3.1   Rugh's Typology of Arab Press

	Mobilization	Loyalist	Diverse	Transitional
Ownership	Government	Private	Private	Mixed
Attitude to regime	Supportive	Supportive	Pro and con	Pro and con
Debate	None	None	Active	Active
Countries	Syria, Libya, The Sudan	Bahrain, Oman, Palestine, Qatar, Saudi Arabia, UAE	Lebanon, Morocco, Kuwait, Yemen, Iraq	Algeria, Egypt, Jordan, Tunisia

Source: Adapted from Rugh (2004:253).

The first system, mobilized press, comprises countries whose governments seek to eliminate all forms of opposition, preferring to utilize the media as part of their revolutionary plans. The second system, loyalist press, includes those countries where the governments do not seek to change the status quo but are content with a passive public. The press, although privately owned, avoids controversial issues rather than seeking to mobilize public opinion. The third system, the diverse press, characterizes the private press fostered in regimes that did not seek to suppress all forms of opposition. In fact, Rugh argues that the diverse press offers the reader "genuine diversity" and enables him to seek the whole story in the different versions and interpretations available in the press: "It can be called the diverse press because its most significant distinguishing characteristic is that the newspapers are clearly different from each other in content and apparent political tendency as well as in style. They are all privately owned and reflect a variety of viewpoints" (2004:87). Finally, the transitional systems include press systems whose future development is not yet clear (Rugh, 2004:134).

Rugh (2004:254) admits, however, that this typology is rather rough and that the Arab press system cannot be divided into neat categories. This typology has also been criticized by Arab scholars for what they see as a lack of theoretical foundation. Al Jammal (2001:150f) points to the fact that all Arab press systems, except Lebanon, are indeed both loyalist and mobilized at the same time. It can be argued that the national newspapers seek to mobilize public opinion, particularly among the well-educated elites, but the party press, as in Egypt, seeks to fulfill the same task while remaining loyal to its political factions. Given that the press has always been related to politics and was even the product of political forces (McFadden, 1953:1), it is therefore predictable that the press fulfills a mobilization mission to a certain extent. The press's dependence on subsidies for survival has also been a reason for journalists' loyalty, albeit temporarily, to certain ideological tendencies (McFadden, 1953; Dajani, 1992).

Arab journalists themselves are aware of the shortcomings of their coverage and the patrimonial policy to which they adhere. Bekhait's (1998) study of Egyptian journalists, for instance, showed that the national journalists admit that their newspapers publish less about scandals and social problems, while journalists in the party press claim they downplay coverage of the positive accomplishments of the government, focusing instead on their respective parties' accomplishments and scandals concerning governmental officials and ministers. The latter declared that scandal news concerning governmental officials and the protocol news about their party leaders should receive less coverage in the future, and the same opinion was expressed by journalists in the national press about their own coverage of governmental activities. Thus, although both groups are essentially loyalist to their benefactors, they may serve as both mobilizing and loyalist tools.

Another critical point about Rugh's typology concerns the third category, "diverse press." Sensenig-Dabbous (2000) argues that the division of the Lebanese "media cake" reflects the political and religious divisions in Lebanon, and that each medium is utilized as a mobilization tool for the faction it serves, and consequently,

> [E]quating the existence of different private broadcast media with pluralism and freedom of expression is a misconception. Though freedom of expression and the media is consecrated for all in the Lebanese Constitution, only those media owned by powerful confessional/economic groups were actually licensed and guaranteed freedom of speech. Weak political, economic, or confessional groups were naturally denied a license and therefore excluded from public debate. (14)

The Lebanese government holds the right to deny licenses to certain press institutions, such as those controlled by Hezbollah, the Phalange, or the Communists (Hafez, 2001:6).

Rugh's typology adheres to the above-mentioned western models relating politics to the press: the totalitarian, communist, and social responsibility models. However, such models have been criticized for not being applicable to developing countries, which are assumed to be in an "in-between" phase that will end in the democratization of their media. Previous research suggests that the Arab media exhibit a combination of features from the totalitarian and developmental models (Nossek & Rinnawi, 2003:185f).

Moreover, it is true that Kuwait enjoys a diversity of newspapers reflecting different orientations, and yet they all agree to show support to the royal family "regardless of their differences" (Kazan, 1994:146). Hafez (2001:5) points out that the Kuwaiti government tightened its grip on the press following the 1991 Gulf War, and journalists themselves have shown a great tendency toward self-censorship. In 2003, the Kuwaiti prime ministry decided to bring charges against the editor-in-chief of *Al Watan* because he criticized a member of the royal family in a public meeting. In his column, the editor attacked the government's decision to enforce a new law that gives the attorney general permission to bring charges against journalists if necessary (*Al Sharq Al Awsat*, 9 June 2003). The Kuwaiti press enjoys great freedom, but when it comes to national affairs, it practices a sort of self-censorship so that the views expressed in the press correspond to those of the royal family. The crown prince allows editors-in-chief to accompany him abroad to keep them abreast of Kuwait's bilateral relations and has meetings with them to discuss urgent Arab issues (*Al Sharq Al Awsa*, 25 January 2001).

On the other hand, other countries, for example the United Arab Emirates (UAE), have regulated their media sector. The Minister of Information and culture in the UAE said in a speech before the Arab Media Club, "The UAE released its grip on the largest media group in the country, Emirates Media Group, which now enjoys independence and freedom to edit what they want. However, they are still dependent on the government's funding" (*Al Bayan*, 4 May 2003)

Abderrahmane (1989:182ff) adds a number of critical points to Rugh's typology, which can be generally summarized in four main arguments:

1. The typology stems from western theories of the press and lacks a critical evaluation of their applicability to the Arab news media. It ignores such questions as how the Arab press reflects the social and cultural traditions of the Arab-Islamic society and how its development might be explained in a new theory apart from those established in western contexts.

2. Rugh's typology suffers a great deal from simplification and generalization; for example, the author mentions that the Arab press, since its birth, has been related to national regimes. This is true in several cases in the Arab world, but some countries deviate from this rule: for instance, Algeria, whose historical roots were distinct from other countries in the region. The press was introduced in Algeria by four different movements: a) the official newspapers representing the French authorities; b) the settlers' press that represented the French inhabitants in Algeria; c) the liberal French press established by French intellectuals who recruited a number of indigenous writers; and d) the national press established by Algerian Muslims.

3. Rugh's typology does not reflect the cultural and social contexts surrounding the Arab press. For instance, Arab countries can be divided according to their cultural heritage into four categories: a) Maghrib countries; b) Nile Valley states; c) Mashreq countries; and d) the Gulf

region. However, Rugh's typology placed countries like Morocco with Kuwait and Lebanon.

4. The typology does not take into account the content of the press, focusing only on one variable, the relationship between the press and government. Rugh is also accused of not adhering to a clearly defined methodology and of ignoring the Palestinian press.

Although Rugh (2004) adds the Palestinian press to this typology, he categorizes it as a "loyalist" press system, although it may also exhibit features of other press systems. Prior to the Oslo Agreement (1993), the Palestinian press represented diverse political interests. Economic support stemmed from four sources: Jordan, the Palestine Liberation Organization (PLO), the Israeli government, and the Israeli Communist Party (Nossek & Rinnawi, 2003:186ff). Only print media existed in the Occupied Territories between 1967 and 1993. The number of newspapers jumped from one in 1968 to forty in 1990. The newspapers were characterized by a variety of ideologies and content. After the Oslo Agreement, the Palestinian press moved to the hands of the Palestinian Authority, whose financial help has been its bread and butter due to the lack of private investment in the sector. Part of this help took the form of advertisements, official notices, and tenders. The media have thus been divided between those partly or wholly dependent on Palestinian Authority subsidies and the rest (Nossek & Rinnawi, 2003:188). Nossek and Rinnawi (2003) conclude their analysis of the Palestinian press by stating that

> Aspects of freedom of the press and censorship mechanisms under Israeli occupation and PA [Palestinian Authority] rule indicate that the formal legislation under the Israeli military resembles the practices of non-democratic regimes, while the PA's laws formally protect freedom of the press. However, if we look at how the respective laws and regulations were implemented, we find a completely different picture. The actual relationship between the PA and Palestinian media is one of harsh (and sometimes violent) control via censorship that is not subject to any kind of judicial or public oversight. As such, the PA interprets its vague press law to impose control on media content through legal and formal forms. As no current PA law legitimizes the existence of a formal censorship organization or mechanism for pre-publication censorship, actual censorship takes place through self-censorship and post-factor publications. (199)

The Palestinian news media is therefore very much the outcome of its political context, the Israeli occupation of the West Bank, Gaza, and Jerusalem since 1967; the Oslo Agreement; and the recurrent *intifada*. News media are a reflection of this political situation. Due to the sensitivity of this situation, Palestinian journalists themselves have been practicing a form of self-censorship, but pressure from the PLO has been exercised even on the news media in diaspora (Al-Khatib, 2002). The Palestinian dailies are said to mirror each other's content, depending on the Palestinian news agency (WAFA) as their main news source instead of relying on their own investigations (Jamal, 2001).

Rugh's typology is thus insufficient to classify Arab media in terms of freedom of speech (Hafez, 2001:6f). On the one hand, the shifting political ideologies in several Arab countries, as in Egypt under Sadat and now under Mubarak, mean that patrimonial systems such as Egypt, Morocco, and Jordan allow more diversity than technocratic systems such as Syria's. On the other hand, it is hard even to generalize about the restrictions imposed on various media, as for instance in Iran, where newspapers are subject to heavy restrictions but magazines are allowed greater diversity (Hafez, 2001:6f). Moreover, developments in the Arab media scene in the last decade call for a new typology in several countries where the governmental establishment has witnessed a shift from older to younger generations (Qatar, Jordan, and Syria) or where the regime has been toppled (Iraq).

In the tiny Gulf monarchy of Qatar, the news satellite channel Al Jazeera has managed to attract the attention of the world media due to its provocative reporting and debates. The channel's correspondents are prohibited from reporting from a number of Arab countries (Bahrain, Jordan, and Saudi Arabia) in protest against the channel's provocative debates on these countries' internal and external affairs. Nevertheless, the internal affairs of Qatar have not received as much attention from Al Jazeera as the affairs of other neighboring countries (El-Nawawy & Iskandar, 2002a) and its seeming freedom does not extend to local media outlets, although Qatar's Emir, Hamed bin Khalifa al-Thani, has taken a number of steps to demonstrate his government's modernization efforts to the world following his bloodless coup in 1995. The establishment of Al Jazeera with a governmental grant was one such initiative. Still, local journalists exercise a great amount of censorship by avoiding criticism of the emir and his policies. The government still controls the issuing of licenses to media outlets and administers penalties for transgression of national and ethical laws imposed on news media: for example, criticizing the emir or printing news that may "harm supreme national interests." In addition, the government controls the distribution of foreign publications in Qatar as well as citizens' access to the Internet.[1]

Following the recent Gulf War, Iraq has not only experienced a changing government but also a changing media scene. After thirty years of work on one assignment, applauding Saddam Hussein's regime, Iraqi media have experienced great diversity and openness. Nevertheless, Iraqi journalists still exercise a form of self-censorship, partly because the current security situation in the country cannot allow for further agitation among the different ethnic and religious factions, and partly because the American coalition forces have not granted complete freedom to Iraqi media.[2] The number of newspapers has exploded in Iraq since the end of the war and there are now 200 publications in Arabic, sixty of them in Baghdad (Soloway, 2003). The Iraqis' hunger for news is also illustrated in the number of TV satellite receivers and the cyber-cafés (twenty in Baghdad) offering unrestricted access to information from the Internet. As one Iraqi shopkeeper put it, "[Iraqis] prefer to spend a bit less on food rather than not have a satellite dish. . . . Even shoemakers are selling them."[3] Those who have access to satellite channels even serve as information providers for others who do not (Leinwand, 2003). The United States has contributed to this information revolution by funding a number of media outlets informing consumers primarily on the coalition forces' activities. Among them is the daily *Al Sabah* (The Dawn) and the Iraqi Media Network (IMN). The American-led coalition has appointed a media commissioner to supervise the media (Leinwand, 2003). The Iraqis have mixed feelings regarding the IMN, whose news production is rather amateurish, using inexperienced, untrained journalists (Soloway, 2003). Iraqis thus have an opportunity not only to watch Arab satellite channels[4] besides channels from neighboring countries, but also foreign channels like CNN and BBC. The diversity of media outlets represents a diversity of ideological tendencies as well, all served at once for an Iraqi media consumer who might be questioning the media's credibility and accuracy.[5] The most credible newspaper, according to the recent report from Reporters without Borders,[6] is *Azzaman*, founded in London in 1996 by a former news media man who fled from Saddam's control. The daily sells around 30,000 copies in Baghdad and prides itself on being a "pluralist paper" (Leinwand, 2003; Reporters without Borders, July 2003).

Rugh maintains that "the occupation authorities from the beginning made it clear that they were determined to establish a democratic political system and a free press, and Iraqi leaders echoed those desires. Iraq's pluralistic society with multiple ethnic and religious divisions made a diverse press natural as long as the central government allowed it. The occupation authorities insisted their control of the country was temporary. As of 2004, therefore, the print media, reflecting the underlying political system, fit quite well into the diverse category" (2004, 117). However, the diversity that the Iraqi media is experiencing at the moment is threatened by lawlessness. Journalists hesitate to write about certain issues lest their writings rile political groups. Although Saddam's control disappeared with the collapse of his regime, the American administration enforces a number of prohibitions on media activities, as in Coalition Provisional Authority Administrator L. Paul Bremer's Order Number Seven to ban reporting that agitates ethnic or religious hatred or violence against the American forces. An anonymous Iraqi journalist has even compared Bremer's policy to Saddam's totalitarian practice of issuing arbitrary decrees. The explosion of newspapers points also to the impalpability of regulations granting licenses to new media outlets in Iraq under the transitional government.[7]

In sum, Rugh's classification is rather vaguely defined, for it does not draw a clear line between mobilization press on the one hand and loyalist press on the other. As the above discussion shows, several countries exhibit features of the diverse press as well. In addition, Rugh seemed to disregard the role of journalists and journalistic culture, which might well differ from one country to another, in the Arab region. For instance, Saudi journalists see their role as preserving and enhancing Islamic values and were content with the notion of employing their talents to achieve the developmental goals of the nation (Tash, 1983). In addition, religious traditions and social background play an important role in forming journalists' values, as Saudi and Algerian journalists suggest (Tash, 1983; Kirat, 1987). Algerian journalists see their mission to be twofold: to educate their readers while working to achieve the goals of the socialist revolution (Kirat, 1987). On the other hand, Egyptian journalists agree that their main mission is to transmit information to the reader rather than to explain events or comment on them. Moreover, Egyptian journalists in the national press agree that they bear a social responsibility toward their country that on one hand forces them to maintain the status quo and on the other may constrain their watchdog role in relation to government officials (Bekhait, 1998:257). The deterioration in the reputation of the press in Egypt and Algeria is attributed to censorship as well as the poor economic situation of the journalists. Conversely, in Saudi Arabia, where journalists receive adequate economic compensation, they tend to assign an important role to their press while overestimating its reputation among their readers. It is then imperative to draw upon the standard of professionalism in the Arab states, which is affected by the journalists' and editors' attitudes toward the news content. Thus, journalists might see their role as educators, mobilizers, informers, or a combination of these. Subsequently, it is important to show how the organizational structure in the newsroom contributes to establishing journalistic standards and practices. In other words, it could be that the political establishment wants to deploy the press as a mobilization tool, but the extent to which this role is fulfilled is subject to the journalistic culture and practices in the country. Finally, it is also important to analyze how journalists see their role in light of their political orientation, historic legacy, and notion of their nation's role.

Another factor is the role of "yellow press" (Abdel Rahman, 2002), which has spread to several Arab countries and assigns itself a role deviating from that of the national press: investigative reporting and provocative journalism. The role of tabloids will be discussed in more detail in chapter four.

Finally, Rugh based his theory mostly on ownership; thus, public ownership of the press would enforce the mobilization role, while private ownership would enforce the loyalist role, and mixed ownership would enforce diversity in content. Now that private ownership is allowed in Egypt, Syria, and Jordan, it can be argued that all these roles are taken up by different media outlets in the same country. That is to say that the Egyptian national press, for instance, would be designated as a mobilization press, while the party press would exhibit features of all the roles, and the independent news media would be classified as diverse. In addition, presuming that the press in some countries plays a mobilization or loyalist role, it is interesting to examine the public's attitude to the information received—especially when they can access foreign news media—and whether the effect of the press on public opinion might be overestimated—particularly with respect to the mobilization function—as there is no evidence of this effect.

Furthermore, it is rather unclear why certain Arab governments would need to maintain an authoritarian press system if the audience is generally well informed and can read between the lines. As Rugh maintains, "Certainly the most sophisticated groups, and to a large extent other people as well, do not accept the news in the mass media entirely at face value, but assume that it may not be completely objective or reliable. They read between the lines, looking for significant omissions and implied meanings." (2004:11). The next section will discuss in more detail the relationship between the press and public opinion in the Arab world.

The Press and Public Opinion

Since the main focus of the news media is on inter-relational and foreign policy issues, it can be argued that its effect will be limited to public opinion on these issues. During wars, for instance, news media play an important role in promoting "an aura of victory." One example is the Iran–Iraq war, where the press in both countries was deployed as an announcement tool, declaring victory while denigrating the enemy without necessarily fulfilling its duty of informing the public of the war's progress (Koeppel, 1989:1). Yet, this does not necessarily mean that the news media are imposing a certain attitude on the public; they may in fact be pandering to its desires. In fact, the American news media that propagated a patriotic tone during the Iraq war won the biggest share of viewership. As an American analyst put it, "Portraying events of the war in a patriotic fashion was drawing in more viewers than a just-the-facts approach" (Sharkey, 2003:18) Reflecting on their own Iraq war coverage, Saudi journalists evaluated the objectivity of their coverage as limited by the public's attitude rather than being capable of influencing it. Some of the Saudi dailies and satellite channels, for instance, sought to follow an "objective" line in the first days of the war but soon abandoned it to attract a larger audience (*Al Sharq Al Awsat,* 18 April 2003).

Moreover, the agenda-setting function of the American news media seems to be confined to foreign policy issues, which distinguishes the United States from the Netherlands, for example, where the news media had very little and rather random effect on public attention to foreign affairs (Schudson, 2003:160). As for domestic affairs, confidence studies among samples of the American news public show the audience's dissatisfaction with the news, a problem that according to Gans (2003:33ff) is rooted in general dissatisfaction with news reports' inaccuracies and coverage that ignores their problems in favor of the interests of the rich. This is one of the similar features between the Arab and American news media. One survey of Saudi civil servants showed that the Saudi media had been effective in setting the international agenda among Saudi citizens, giving them ideas of "what to think about" (Al Haqeel & Melkote, 1995:34). However, when it comes to setting the agenda for domestic affairs, there was a huge discrepancy between the media's agenda and the public's agenda: the news media followed the "official" line in avoiding reporting on controversial topics like the cost of living, social problems, and religion, regardless of the fact that these were the very issues that respondents ranked at the top of their personal agenda (Al Haqeel & Melkote, 1995:32).[8]

The indulgence in foreign policy issues is not only deeply rooted in the history of news reporting in the Arab region but also in officials' attitudes toward the news media, which it sees primarily as a foreign policy tool. The Egyptian Minister of Information has, for instance, criticized the Arab news media for failing to work on consolidation strategies with other channels and newspapers or international news agencies that were offered for sale, instead allowing the "Zionist" media to control the western news media outlets and thereby promote its ideologies (*Al Bayan,* 25 October 2002). An editorial in *Al Sharq Al Awsat* has called for Arab investors to buy stock in CNN, whose share price was in constant decline in the wake of the September 11th attacks, thus ensuring a share of the media power, which is seen to exceed that of nuclear weapons (Abu Khadra, 2003).

Public opinion is said to have more influence on the party press in Egypt than vice versa. Yet, the Arab party press lacks one important factor for flourishing as an alternative medium: professional journalists. Most of the journalists writing for the party press are leading members of the party and not professional journalists. The ideologies reflected in these writings belong to the leading figures of the party and do not therefore reflect the diversity of views among ordinary members. Thus, the party press has not functioned as a platform for exchanging opinions but rather as a propaganda tool in the hands of their leading members, whose focus on issues has oscillated with public opinion in all areas.[9]

According to the first Arab study investigating the agenda-setting role of the media (Hamada, 1993), the media has little effect on the public opinion. Nonetheless, the print press was given a far more important role than the electronic media, probably because the latter have been assigned other functions, primarily entertainment, that reduce their agenda-setting capability. Hamada (1993:296ff) points to several reasons for this, among them the lack of information available to the public to participate politically and its impotence in translating its resentment into political action. In addition, opinion polls have not been applied as successful tools to measure public opinion on political and social issues, partly because of the restrictions surrounding this kind of research and partly because of the biases of the researchers themselves.

In addition, the vast number of Arabic-language publications established in foreign capitals have readership inside the Arab region. Some of the publications are sponsored by Arab regimes, Libya for instance, and others are semi-independent. A few—like *Al Sharq Al Awsat* and *Al Hayat*—now claim a pan-Arab role. The émigré press is not a new phenomenon, dating back only a quarter century, as Rugh maintains (2004:167). In fact, its roots go back to the end of the nineteenth century. Rugh's categorization does not directly account for the role this type of press plays in public opinion; that is, offering a diversity of opinion or simply fulfilling a mobilizing or loyalist role for certain regimes. The following section addresses the issue of the émigré press.

Arab Newspapers Abroad

The last three decades have witnessed the phenomenon of pan-Arab newspapers published outside the region, such as in London and Paris. This phenomenon is not new, though; it began in the nineteenth century when a number of Arab newspapers were founded outside the region (Abu Zeid, 1993) by émigrés fleeing the political and economic situations in their homelands. The second wave includes newspapers established from the middle of the 1970s. In his comparison between the first and second waves, Abu Zeid (1993:454ff) identifies similarities such as the fact that the first wave publications appeared during the period of colonization of the region and were used by the colonial powers in an attempt to win public opinion. Among these publications were *Mira't Al Ahwal* (Mirror of Events), issued in London and recruited for service to the British Empire, and the pro-French *Berjis*

Baris (Paris Jupiter). Although the second-wave publications were founded following the independence of the Arab states, they served the same political goal in the hands of the Arab regimes, which have used them in their ideological and political rivalries. Among the differences between them are several factors. While the first wave was mostly comprised of Egyptian, Lebanese, and Syrian publications, the second wave was comprised of publications representing other countries in the region. The first wave included publications by those that fled to other regions as well as those fleeing the ethnic and religious conflicts in their own countries but remaining in the region: for example, the Lebanese and Syrian journalists who migrated to Egypt under the British occupation in the nineteenth century. The second wave, however, was confined to migration outside the Arab region. The first-wave publications were first and foremost political in nature, serving the political and ideological purposes of their founders and benefactors, while the second wave was comprised of specialized publications, such as women's, cultural, and sports magazines (Abu Zeid, 1993:454ff).

Al Jammal (2001:128) argues that there exists no one newspaper that can call itself all "Arabs' newspaper" because, as he argues elsewhere, there are a number of differences among the Arab states and thus it is more correct to describe a newspaper according to the ideologies or national interests it represents. Likewise, categorizing all Arabic newspapers issued from outside the region as the "émigré press" is a misconception (Al Jammal, 2001:134; Abu Zeid, 1993:448ff). The Arab newspapers issued from European capitals can be divided into three types (Al Jammal, 2001:134ff):

1. Newspapers founded by Arabs who immigrated to other regions for the purpose of consolidating their relations with their home countries. Such newspapers do not adhere to political ideologies or serve national interests, but are usually specialized publications serving religious, cultural, or social purposes. Examples are the number of publications founded by the Yemenis residing in Indonesia and Singapore or those published by the Lebanese in Latin America.
2. Newspapers and publications founded by national media institutions abroad to serve as an extended arm to national propaganda. Some of these publications have also moved outside the Arab region for technical and marketing reasons: *Al Sharq Al Awsat,* for example.
3. Newspapers that had to move outside the region due to the deterioration of the security situation in their home countries are the only types that deserve to be called "émigré press." Among these publications are those of the Lebanese that had to immigrate to London, Paris, Cyprus, and other places, fleeing from the civil wars in Lebanon (1975–1990).

In his comprehensive analysis of Arab newspapers published outside the region, Abu Zeid (1993:448ff) rejects categorizing them as "international" publications since they do not conform to the definition of international publication: 1) international distribution; 2) great effect inside and outside the region; and 3) the usage of one language widely shared by a great number of readers outside the national boundaries, or alternatively, publishing in several language editions. The third factor has enabled English-speaking publications to be regarded as international due to the dominance of English as a lingua franca. Modern Standard Arabic (MSA), despite the fact that it is the common language of 160 million Arabs[10] inside the Arab region, cannot be regarded as an international language, and thus Arabic language publications aim only at the Arabic-speaking communities inside or outside the region. Hence, they hardly have the great effect on the international scene that English-language publications do. Abu Zeid (1993:453) argues that even those newspapers that call themselves "international editions," such as *Al Ahram International* (Egypt) or *Qabas International* (Kuwait), should rather be called "Arab editions" since their content does not differ from the "regional editions."

Abu Zeid (1993:470) concludes his study of such publications by hypothesizing that the less media freedom there is in a country, the more media will be obligated to flee. Other scholars, however, do not agree that the diaspora press has much freedom, because "the arm of the state is a long one" (Koeppel, 1989:1).

Nevertheless, the reasons that drove these newspapers abroad—lack of technology, access to information, and censorship—seem to have diminished, as several pan-Arab newspapers are now returning to the Arab world. Although censorship is still practiced in one way or another in the Arab states, the technological progress and the information revolution the region is experiencing are providing a suitable basis for these newspapers to operate from the Arab world (Ghareeb, 2000).

It is then safe to assume that the émigré press does in fact fulfill several functions: mobilization, serving certain regimes; diversity, offering pluralistic opinions; information and commercial via specialized publications. Also, one country may sponsor different media outlets, each serving a different function, as in the Saudi-sponsored press.

To sum up, Rugh's categorization of the Arab press, although it represents one of the few comprehensive studies available, exhibits a number of shortcomings that make it difficult to apply the typology at its face value. In my view, there are three main shortcomings in the typology: 1) it ignores the role of journalists and their traditions and socialization in light of the new developments on the Arab media scene; 2) it does not account for the role of the offshore or émigré press and how it fits into the suggested typology; and 3) Rugh implies bias against Arab journalism, as will be discussed later. For instance, Rugh (1987:165) argued that Arab journalists might succeed in escaping strict governmental control when backed by powerful political factions. The Egyptian party press has succeeded in escaping the "official" line of journalism but has fallen instead under the strict policy of the political parties. Also, the political culture in the Arab region does not necessarily pull in the direction of free, critical journalism as in the United States. This can be illustrated by the Saudi journalists' disinterest in establishing their own press union and their acceptance of having such a union under the auspices of the government (Tash, 1983). Besides, the rough categorization of the Saudi press as loyalist does not account for the Saudi business tycoons' establishment of media outlets that seek to stir Arab public opinion on political and social issues rather than maintaining the status quo.

According to Rugh's classification, Arab governments exercise great power, particularly in mobilization and loyalist systems, in specifying media policies for the press. But this rules out the role of journalists and how they conceive their role in society. They may, for instance, aspire to lift up their professional reputation and standards by modernizing their news production even under strict censorship on the part of the state. Mohammed H. Heikal, the former editor-in-chief of the Egyptian *Al Ahram*, managed, for instance, to get away with criticizing the government openly in his commentaries, relying on his good relations with the former president Abdel Nasser, who in fact consulted him on various political matters (Nasser, 1979). Thus, the classification of the Arab press into four categories depending on the censorship exercised by the government does not account for the symbiotic relationship that takes place between the three actors involved in news production: government, journalists/editors, and the audience. Rather, the government is granted the major role in this relationship insofar as it on the one hand controls what the journalists publish and on the other controls what the audience gets, as illustrated in figure 3.1.

According to this model, the audience is cornered by two controlling parties: the government that controls the flow of information and the press that

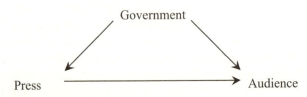

Figure 3.1   Authoritarian Press System

controls the content of the news they access. However, the audience normally has access to other news output, such as foreign media, or at least the Arabic-language service in foreign media such as the BBC and Voice of America. Also, the foreign media has a professional effect on the journalists/editors in that they serve as an inspirational source for the journalists' modernization initiatives. In addition, the mobilization classification implies that the government controls the content of newspapers and television newscasts by dictating media policies. This is rather incorrect, as Algerian journalists, for instance, complain of a lack of clear media policies on the part of the government (Kirat, 1987). Instead, the government makes laws that define the limits of the press—what journalists should not write about—rather than laws that define what they should write about. Within the limits of freedom granted by the government, party press and independent press function in several Arab states, even though all journalists are subject to the same laws and penalties. The press, on the other hand, pushes the limits of freedom as far as it can. The party press focuses on scandals (Bekhait, 1998), adopting the role of watchdog, while the national press adopts the role of social responsibility by focusing on the positive accomplishments of the government. The independent press, moreover, operates on market logic: their supply is subject to the demand of their audience, be it internal political conflict, celebrity gossip, scandal, or corruption.

Another actor in the above model, the audience, also exercises a form of power over the press. The audience seeks to read about popular internal issues, which is why the tabloids are more successful in several Arab states, notably Egypt. The audience seeks service information such as classified ads, and that is why *Al Ahram*, for instance, dedicates a large part of the newspaper to this service. They also provide entertainment sections, which is why Ramadan sales are higher compared to sales figures for the rest of the year. On normal days, the audience drops newspapers and depends on regular television newscasts for news; in times of crisis, newspaper circulation increases tremendously.[11]

Moreover, Rugh's categorization, although updated three times during the past twenty-five years, still does not account for new developments on the Arab media scene. Take for example Rugh's claim about the few journalism schools in the Arab world: "Schools of journalism are few and recently established, so most media staff have learned their trade on the job" (1987:12). In 2004, Rugh still maintains the same assumption, albeit with a slight revision: "Schools of journalism are few, so most media staff have learned their trade on the job" (2004:11). It is quite implausible that the situation of journalism schools has not changed a lot during almost two decades. Figures from the 1980s (Abdel Rahman, 1991) pointed to the existence of thirty institutions spread in seventeen

Arab countries. Egypt and Saudi Arabia had the major share of these schools, with six and five schools, respectively. Cairo University, however, is the only academic institution that offers both master's and PhD degrees. In addition, she asserted that the percentage of the total number of journalists who had university degrees in communications was around 60 percent (Abdel Rahman, 1989:78), and the same results were confirmed in other studies among Arab journalists (e.g., Kirat, 1987, and Tash, 1983).

Rugh's (2004) presentation seems furthermore to suffer from some unfortunate generalizations and biases, such as his bias against the Arabic language and its "poetic" nature and the effect of this on the journalistic product. For instance, he argues, "There is an 'intimate interdependence' between Arabic and the Arab psychology and culture, and, thus, as carriers of the language, the mass media are very important in the communication of Arab cultural commonality . . . Arabic is filled with what speakers of English would consider exaggeration and repetition" (19). This overstatement is due to classical myths about the role of the classical or written form of Arabic, as discussed in more detail in chapter six. Rugh takes this overstatement as far as using it as a yardstick against which he compares Arab versus American journalists' reporting style by stating, "Whereas the American journalist seems to have a passion for factual details and statistics, the Arab journalist by contrast seems to give more attention to the correct words, phrasing, and grammar he should use in describing an event" (19). If his assumption about American journalists' negligence of language details is correct, then that might explain why more than two-thirds of American readers complain of the grammatical and language errors in the contemporary American press (see the survey conducted by the American Society of Newspaper Editors, 1999).[12]

This subtle comparison between Arab and American journalistic standards continues in Rugh's (2004) categorization of the Arab press. For instance, he argues,

> There are newspapers which have achieved reputations for relative objectivity in news reporting, although their columnists are known for their various political biases. But typically the news treatment as well as the commentaries of a newspaper or broadcasting station will be regarded by the audience with a large measure of defensive skepticism, akin to that of Americans toward a commercial advertisement . . . The credibility for the news writers and political columnists in the media tends to be lower than in the West . . . Journalism ranks relatively low in prestige except for the handful of prominent columnists in each country, usually fewer than a half dozen, who write the signed political analyses that appear in the daily press." (11)

Later he resumes, "It is also true that many news stories in Arab media do not entirely measure up to the ideal that some have set for the American press, for example, of a 'truthful, comprehensive, and intelligent account of the day's events in a context which gives them meaning'" (Rugh, 2004:17).

Now, Rugh raises two issues here. The first is the lack of credibility and respectability enjoyed by professional journalists in the Middle East compared to the West (United States), and the second is that Arab journalistic practices are still far from the American ideal of objectivity and truthfulness.

Let us take the first issue: Several western scholars have disputed the truthful account of daily news, ideally claimed by the "free" American press. According to Hachten (1999:144), for instance, news from the 1991 Gulf War was controlled by American military leaders who often "held back" some important information or even twisted the facts they released publicly. For instance, the pride of using smart bombs that hit their targets with 90 percent accuracy was soon replaced with the Air Force confession that such bombs were only 7 percent of all the explosives used in the war and that 70 percent of them missed their targets. The problem of credibility is not confined to less democratic press systems. American newspapers, for example, have witnessed a remarkable decrease in their readership since the 1980s, which was justified by Meyer (1988:567) to be the result of the decreasing credibility of the news offered in newspapers. Moreover, according to the survey published by the Center for Media and Public Affairs (1997), only a small majority of American readers believe that the news media actually prints accurate facts, while more than 35 percent think that the news media have not been careful in correcting errors in their news reporting. The majority believe that the media are biased in favor of one side of the story, and a large majority also believe that the news is politically biased. They also expressed concern that the news media were often influenced by the opinions of powerful people or organizations, not to mention their view of journalists as "arrogant, cynical and less compassionate" than most people.[13]

Secondly, the objectivity that Rugh claims prevails in more democratic press systems, particularly the American system, is not a normative system that the less free systems should aspire to; rather, it is a set of norms or objectifying "devices" that may vary from one journalistic tradition to another. Westerståhl (1983:403) regards the use of the word "objectivity" as unfortunate since it is at the heart of the larger discussions about the nature of knowledge, a problem disputed by philosophers for centuries. Thus, the claim of the news media to rely on "objectivity" in news reporting is merely an indication of their adherence to certain norms. For instance, Zelizer, Park, and Gudelunas (2002:291) argue that among the objectifying devices used by the mainstream U.S. media were the use of facts or figures, graphics, and other visual aids. American news media, in particular, have witnessed a move from being overwhelmingly descriptive in the 1960s to being predominantly interpretive

in the 1990s (Patterson, 1993:82). This move, according to a number of scholars, has resulted in a more biased journalism. For instance, Zelizer, Park, and
Gudelunas (2002) examined the coverage of the *intifada* during thirty days in
the mainstream U.S. newspapers (the *New York Times*, the *Washington Post*,
and the *Chicago Tribune*). They maintain that the normative assumption
about journalism is that it should hold an objective and neutral stance with
regard to events it reports upon and that this has been in decline as untenable
norm as scholars have unraveled the bias in journalists' coverage (Zelizer,
Park, & Gudelunas, 2002:284). They argue, in line with other researchers, that
several aspects of the Palestinian/Israeli conflict were absent in the American
media, such as how Israeli soldiers treat Palestinians, while these aspects were
covered in other media, such as the British and the Israeli media (Zelizer, Park,
& Gudelunas, 2002:287). In addition, the pro-Israeli perspective in the U.S.
news media derived from their failure to provide a historical context for the
coverage and thereby little explanation of the Palestinian reactions. They concluded, "Bias thus emerges as a far more embedded and complex dimension
of U.S. print journalism than commonly assumed in popular, if not in scholarly, discourse" (Zelizer, Park, & Gudelunas, 2002:302). One American editor
justified the shortcoming in the coverage of the Middle East by the lack of
knowledge about the region: "I think what was wrong with American coverage of the Middle East in the past was not so much a lack of objectivity, whatever that means, but really a lack of enterprise and imagination. It wasn't so
much that everybody was pro-Israel—although, of course, there was great
sentiment for Israel—but it was that we weren't really interested enough in the
Arab world. There was a vast area of ignorance. We didn't have enough . . . correspondents in the area" (Rubin, 1979:228). Thus, the presentation of this
region in the American news media has not always been balanced, but rather
biased in times when it is desperately needed to ensure the public's understanding of American policy there (Barranco & Shyles, 1988:178).

　　Generally, the shortcomings might be due to Rugh's negligence of the available body of research written by Arab scholars in Arabic. This is an ethical
issue for any researcher, namely to present the "other" view as well, particularly if they master the "other" language, as William Rugh is said to master
Arabic. Rugh says, for instance, "This book, however, does not present a comprehensive qualitative survey of media content. The above observations about
content are made on the basis of opinions of experienced consumers of these
media and not on the basis of an objective and systematic content analysis of
press, radio, and television in all eighteen countries. Such a study has not yet
been done, and would be an enormous undertaking" (2004:250). Albeit laud-
able, this statement certainly ignores the vast amount of studies on Arab news
media presented in Arabic and English by Arab scholars (e.g., Abu Zeid

(1993), Al Jammal (1990), Abdel Rahman (1989, 2002), Moaw'ad (2000), El Sarayrah (1986), Bekhait (1998), Abdel Nabi (1989), Ayish (2001a), and Al Abd (1995), to mention but a few!).

Abdel Rahman (2002:32ff) offers an alternative to Rugh's typology, namely a thematic typology of the Arab press. She defines the themes that occupied the Arab countries during the 1950s and 1960s as revolving around Arab unity and the Israeli conflict, which motivated the mobilization function of the press. During the 1970s, development issues and fighting dependency were the main concerns in the region, which promoted the loyalist function of the press. In the 1980s, Arabs' attention was directed to other immediate issues, such as democracy and cultural imperialism and the effect of the oil wealth on the Arab culture. Finally, the 1990s witnessed the increased interest in human rights and preparing the region for the information revolution, thus promoting the diverse role of the news media (Ayish, 2001b:114f).

Alternatively, Ayish (2002b) provides a more qualified categorization of Arab communication patterns: traditional government-controlled, reformist government-controlled, and liberal commercial patterns. The first pattern comprises traditional communication channels: for example, the Syrian Satellite Channel, which, despite the progress it has made in its entertainment production, still follows the traditional editorial orientation in its news output. The second pattern is demonstrated by channels such as Abu Dhabi, where journalistic professionalism has been markedly elevated to compete with other news channels. Generally, such channels seek to balance professional aspirations with the cultural and political contexts in which they operate. Finally, the third pattern refers to channels such as Al Jazeera, where professional rather than political interest is the driving force behind news selection and gathering. However, it should be stressed that Ayish's model is still a rough one. For instance, the third pattern cannot be characterized as "commercial" when the state of Qatar is the main financial patron of Al Jazeera, and it is still debatable whether the channel is really journalistically free when critics accuse it of ignoring Qatari internal affairs. Moreover, the channel has been part of the Qatari emir's plans to modernize his state and direct the world's attention to it. Whether Al Jazeera will keep being a part of these plans or will lead the way toward a free journalistic tradition in the Arab region is still too early to judge. The traditional communications system still characterizes countries like Libya, where no reform or modernization plans have been set out in the media sector. The reformist system refers to one or more segments of the news media within one country. Thus, the party press in Egypt, for instance, is reformist in that it seeks to deviate from the traditional role of the national press, while the independent press (tabloids) can be characterized as a commercial system, driven only by market logic and the demands of their audience.

Instead of categorizing the Arab press and news media according to ownership, it is more important to consider other factors, such as content. The government's financial control of these media institutions, for instance, does not
necessarily make them less free or less critical of the regime. There are several
public service media institutions in Western Europe, and their critical stance
toward their governments is as obvious as it is in commercial systems such as
the American system (Benson, 2001). Furthermore, Rugh's typology seems to
focus on what Bourdieu (1990) refers to as the political "field," where the focus
is on the government's degree of interference in the news media through ownership. In so doing, the discussion rules out other important factors, such as
market logic, journalistic practices, and the cultural context. However, by considering the content of the news media, and not only the ownership, it be-
comes clearer how these factors play a role in the development of the Arab
news media.

As discussed elsewhere, political news, particularly foreign news, prevails
in Arab news media. However, the new satellite channels, with their emphasis on entertainment programs, as well as the increasing size of culture sections in some pan-Arab newspapers, such as *Al Hayat*, must be accounted for
in a new categorization. Figure 3.2 illustrates such a categorization.

The figure shows news media plotted against two axes, the degree of political and cultural content:

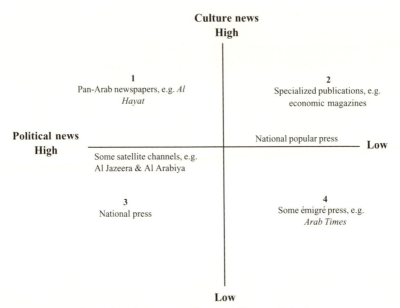

Figure 3.2   Typology of Arab News Media According to Their Content

1. The first type includes publications such as the so-called pan-Arab press (e.g., *Al Hayat* and *Al Sharq Al Awsat*), where the political focus is still high but is balanced by the increasing amount of cultural news.
2. The second type includes very specialized publications (e.g., economic or literary publications) targeting particular segments of the Arab audience. On the border between "high culture" and "low politics," one can locate the national popular press or the so-called yellow press, since it centers on local events related to a specific cultural context and not necessarily on appealing to a pan-Arab audience.
3. The third type includes national press, where the cultural sections and news are lower priorities compared to political news. Some new satellite channels (e.g., Al Jazeera) can be placed on the border between "high politics" and "low culture," since they devote most of their content to (foreign) political issues, although interest in cultural and local issues has grown recently.
4. The fourth type includes various types of émigré popular press (e.g., the *Arab Times*), which Arab scholars prefer to call the yellow press, where the content centers more around personal issues than political issues.

Furthermore, these media institutions may differ among themselves in whether they target national or regional audiences. Usually, the popular or yellow press, for example, in Egypt and Jordan, is characterized by an abundance of light news with a local angle. However, some émigré newspapers, such as the *Arab Times*,[14] depend on light news from different Arab countries, thus addressing a larger segment of readers. The pan-Arab news media outlets, such as the *Al Hayat* and *Al Sharq Al Awsat* newspapers and the Al Jazeera and Abu Dhabi satellite channels, address a wider audience and their news therefore has a regional angle. Protocol and propaganda-like news is here replaced with foreign news involving several Arab states. The profit margin does not necessarily have to be in monetary value, but could also be in purchasing "goodwill" or enhancing the image of the country hosting a particular media outlet, such as the state of Qatar, which hosts Al Jazeera.

In terms of the economic value of each type, the first and second types might be regarded as adhering to market logic insomuch as they seek to attract a larger audience and thus more advertisers. Because it addresses pre-defined and limited segments of the Arab audience, the second type might be more successful in attracting advertisers who target exactly the same segments of "consumers." This does not mean, however, that the quality of the content of these specialized publications is less genuine. The third type adheres to media logic, in that it focuses on the larger issues of importance to several countries of the region, such as foreign policy issues. The media logic then refers to the way in which these news organizations define what is newsworthy and how it should be formulated. Finally, the fourth type aims at attracting a larger audience and thereby advertisers, but the resources available in terms of financial and human or journalistic resources may not be sufficient to achieve this goal.

The above model can be applied as a tool in empirical research focusing on the content of news media and how this content reflects changes in a number of factors in the Arab media scene, such as journalistic practices, organizational situations in the news media, news values or ethics, and relations to sources. For instance, research can trace the (diachronic and synchronic) changes in news content in terms of the division between hard and soft news and how this has affected the news values adhered to by media institutions and by individual journalists. Other significant factors can be the relationship between news media outlets and advertisers on the one hand and the role of the audience in the development of media content on the other hand or the relationship between journalists and their sources and the hierarchy of sources used in both hard and soft news. This line of research can be anchored in sociological theories, such as Bourdieu's (1984, 1990). Bourdieu's research offers a framework to study journalism as a social field in accordance with other fields in society, such as the political and economic fields. One of the focal issues in this theory is the analysis of the distribution of power in a particular field. Following this model, the Arab press can be presented as a hierarchal system composed of the so-called serious versus yellow press, magazines versus newspapers, pan-Arab versus national/local dailies, and so forth. The elements within the systems are separated only by symbolic barriers created by the amount of "capital" assigned to each element. A hierarchal system also exists among journalists reflecting their professional, editorial, academic, and symbolic power, values, and reflexivity. Moreover, the role of the media language (MSA) should be analyzed as part of the symbolic power assigned to each journalist.

To summarize, this chapter has presented a categorization of Arab press according to four different variables:

1. ownership;
2. central topics of the news;
3. ownership and news format; and
4. content.

Rugh's (1987, 2004) typology uses one primary variable, namely ownership, to categorize the Arab press into four main categories: mobilized, loyalist, diverse, and transitional. However, whether the state owns the press or if it is owned by private organization(s) may prove to have little specific effect upon its content. One example of this is Al Jazeera, which is financed by the state emir, but nonetheless has been classified as a "commercial" channel (Ayish, 2002b) because of the new angles it has introduced in terms of style, genre, techniques, and topics. Furthermore, Rugh classifies some private media outlets as "loyalist" according to whether they adhere to the policies of the ruling government or regime. This classification, however, does not account for the paradox of the presence of private-owned media outlets that have not sought to simply enforce the existing policies. In fact, some pan-Arab newspapers, such as the Saudi-owned *Al Sharq Al Awsat*, tried to conceal their sources of finance to stress their neutrality, even to the extent of ignoring the news from Saudi Arabia altogether (Abu Zeid, 1993:222). Likewise, if the loyalist media outlets aim to preserve the status quo and enforce existing policies and traditions, then how can we explain the paradoxical situation where wealthy Arabs, particularly Saudi businessmen, finance satellite channels that largely depend on beautiful young hostesses to attract the audience (Al Kadry & Harb, 2002), or on certain types of entertainment programs that serve the same purpose (and which a prominent Arab journalist even dubbed "soft porn") (al-Kasim, 1999), if these values directly contradict Saudi traditions and cultural values? In fact, it can be argued that the driving force behind the establishment of new media outlets is purely commercial, as these media are expected to generate and maximize return on investments (as finances or image). Thus content is dictated by what the public wants, or what the media people think the public wants, or in otherwise building or maintaining a certain image that contributes indirectly to the profit margin.

In contrast to Rugh's (1987, 2004) typology, Abdel Rahman (2002) prefers to categorize the press according to the news topics, which were central between the 1950s and the 1990s, be they Arab unity, modernization, or other related topics. Ayish (2002b) presents a third alternative by categorizing modern Arab news media, particularly the new satellite channels, into three categories: traditionalist, reformist, and commercial.

Here, a fourth taxonomy is proposed, dividing the media according to content. This differs from the previous three theories insomuch as the news media is divided according to the content of the news. This division, moreover, takes into account the commercial purposes that these media serve, whether it is to generate as large a profit as possible or to contribute to building a new image and hence goodwill for a particular country or media outlet.

Notes

1. See www.cpj.org/attacks02/mideast02/qatar.html
2. See the Reporters Without Borders report on Iraq: The Iraqi media three months after the war: A new but fragile freedom. Available online: www.rsf.org

3. Reporters Without Borders report on Iraq.

4. A poll conducted among Iraqis in the period between 28 August and 4 September 2003 showed that they prefer Al Arabiya to Al Jazeera and other satellite channels. Al Arabiya won 59 percent of the votes for its "objectivity" in war coverage, while Al Jazeera got 40 percent of the votes, Abu Dhabi 29 percent, and the Iraqi US-supported media outlet IMN received 24 percent. At the bottom of the list were the BBC at 6 percent and CNN at 2 percent. Nevertheless, the Iraqis placed Al Arabiya and Al Jazeera, plus several other Arab satellite channels, at the top of the list of channels that were biased in favor of both the American side and Saddam's regime. Source: *Al Sharq Al Awsat*, 13 November 2003, Iraqi viewers prefer Al Arabiya to Al Jazeera.

5. Leinwand (2003) quotes a number of Iraqi citizens who expressed skepticism over what the media report. As one of them put it, "The majority of the local press are lying. The newspapers in Saddam's day were lying as well. So we are used to it."

6. Reporters Without Borders: The Iraqi media three months after the war: A new but fragile freedom. Available online at www.rsf.org

7. See the Reporters Without Borders report on Iraq.

8. Al Haqeel & Melkote (1995) chose to confine their research to civil servants because access to this segment is easy since home delivery of mail does not exist in Saudi Arabia and the best place to reach respondents is at their work place.

9. Al Doury, Wifaq H. Tabii'at alsahafa al hizbiya wa tatowiroha (Nature of party press and its development). Downloaded from the site of Arab research on mass media, at http.:t1t.net/89s.htm

10. According to Suleiman (2003), Arabic is a common language for another 140 million.

11. According to a Saudi newsstand, people buy not only their favorite newspaper but also a variety of others—on average three newspapers during the recent Iraq war. In Morocco, the manager of the Moroccan distribution company said that circulation increased slightly around four days before the war began, which was why his company has asked the Moroccan newspapers to increase their printing capacity by 20 percent. He recalled the situation during the 1991 Gulf War, when Moroccan newspapers increased their circulation by 40 percent. Yet, he does not expect the same situation to repeat itself during the current war, simply because of the ubiquitous presence of Arab TV-satellite channels sending live reports from the battlefield. The major Moroccan newspaper, *Al Ahdath Al Maghribiya*, increased its circulation from 95,000 to 103,000 a day, and *Al Alam* increased from 60,000 to 89,000 a day. Nevertheless, Moroccan newspapers usually do not have correspondents in Iraq or the neighboring countries. Source: *Al Sharq Al Awsat*, 25 March 2003, Saudi citizens reorganize their priorities & Moroccan newspapers increase their circulation: 14.

12. www.asne.org/kiosk/reports/99reports/1999examiningourcredibility/

13. Center for Media and Public Affairs (September 1997). What the People Want from the Press. Executive Summary: www.cmpa.com/archive/wdtpwftp.htm (15 August 2003).

14. Established in 1986, *Arab Times* is published every ten days. Its editor-in-chief is the Palestinian-born Osama Fawzi. For more information, see the newspaper's website at www.arabtimes.com.

4

News Values

THE CRITERIA JOURNALISTS USE FOR selecting the news vary from one culture to another, reflecting various ideological, political, and cultural realities. In other words, what might be regarded as news in an Arab country may not necessarily be newsworthy to an American media outlet, and vice versa. Indeed, the concept of news and newsworthiness might even differ from one Arab country to another. Unfortunately, Arab news values have not received sufficient attention from academia, except from a few studies. According to an early study of the Arab press (McFadden, 1953:66), national news with an Arab angle constituted around fifty percent of the news in Arab dailies, while soft news and editorials represented twelve percent and seven percent, respectively. One study of Arab news values during the 1970s (Abu Bakr, 1980:21) pointed to the theme of pan-Arabism at the top of factors influencing the selection of news at the time. Ideologies propagating anti-imperialism as well as development plans formed other influential factors in news selection. Another study (Dajani, 1989) defined two crucial factors for news selection in the Arab press: the relationship between national authorities and the news sources and geographical proximity. The latter factor influenced even news reporting on Arab affairs. Thus, North African news was rather absent from the Gulf press, and likewise the Gulf news was rather absent from the Lebanese and Egyptian press. The findings suggested a range of news values according to the political orientation in each country. Thus, the Algerian press paid great attention to development news, aiming at educating rather than informing readers. The Egyptian press, on the other hand, focused on protocol news, exaggerating the positive role of governmental policies. The Lebanese press demonstrated a diversity of opinions, but it could not be claimed that it played a watchdog role. Among the similar values shared by the Arab press were a decline of soft news and an abundance of news aimed at urban readers, with the exception of the Saudi press, where each region enjoyed its own (elite) newspapers. Nasser (1983) confirmed the tendency of Third World journalists to conceive of their role as educators rather than informers.

More recent studies on news values in the Arab region (Turkistani, 1989:215ff; Abdel Nabi, 1989) point to the criteria of proximity (geographical and cultural), protocol news, and personification as among the major values in Arab news media. Abdel Nabi (1989) added to that the criterion of social responsibility, meaning that the selection of news is bound to preserving the society's moral and religious beliefs. The press should then work to maintain national unity by not stirring ethnic or religious conflict.

In the West, an earlier study (Ostgaard, 1965:45ff) pointed to three main factors that influenced the flow of news: simplification, identification, and sensationalism. Another study (Golding & Elliott, 1979) suggested proximity, negativity, entertainment, and prominence or personification as major factors. The most influential study on western news values dates back to 1965 in an article by the Norwegian researchers Galtung and Ruge (1973) that pointed to certain criteria as the most essential in news selection regardless of the cultural context: proximity, frequency, meaningfulness, unexpectedness, prominence, and negativity. The theory was criticized by various researchers, who questioned its empirical validity—pointing to the generalization of the theory, which made it hard for researchers to apply it to the study of news flow—and its theoretical foundations, which were criticized as eclectic (Hjarvard, 1992).

Recent studies and journalistic handbooks (e.g., Fedler et al., 1997) suggest proximity, importance, identification, and newness as major news values in the western news media. These criteria are similar to those mentioned in the Arab research cited above, with the exception of identification, since most of the news is said to be hard, protocol news, with which the readers cannot easily identify. In this chapter, news values in contemporary Arab media will be discussed, focusing on four major criteria: abundance of political news, the social responsibility of the news, prominence, and newness. The choice of these values is based on a review of current literature (e.g., Abdel Nabi, 1989; Abu Zeid, 1993; Bekhait, 1998; Schudson, 2003). A comparative approach is adopted to help locate the similarities and differences between American and Arab news values. Moreover, the notion of objectivity, and to what extent both Arab and American journalism adhere to it, will also be discussed.

News Is Politics

Already in the eighteenth century, American newspeople realized the importance of political news to their readers. The amount of such news increased both in quantity and quality. Proceedings of the House of Representatives were part of the news diet in the United States in 1789 (Green, 2002:40) and news served a greater role in the public sphere at that time.

American news of the nineteenth century was mostly political news, and newspeople were mainly occupied with reviewing official, formal procedures (Schudson, 1978). This tendency did not hold long into the twentieth century: political (hard) news was reduced in favor of soft news. This is one finding of the analysis of newspapers from 1977 through 1997 conducted by the American Committee of Concerned Journalists. The committee showed that human-interest news has been on the increase, while political and foreign news has been in decline (Kock, 2002:26). Williston (2001) summarizes the reasons for this. The commercialization of the American media forced media outlets to compete for profit, particularly in the 1980s and early 1990s after the issuing of the Television Act, which minimized the role of public service broadcasting. To compete for the largest share of audience ratings, the stations had to cut down on the costly production of news and increase entertainment. As a result of commercialization and the fierce competition among channels, the networks had to cut the cost of foreign news and correspondents' expenditures abroad. It was enough to use a pooling service, where one camera provides all networks with the same footage. The emergence of CNN as a 24-hour channel with breaking news as a specialty further forced the networks away from competition on news. Thus, breaking news and big stories are now left to CNN to cover.

American newspapers in the colonial era and early republic structured their news beginning with the most important events occurring in other capitals and ending with local items from American states. This, however, is exactly the opposite of modern practice, where local events have moved to the front page and international news to inside pages (Barnhurst & Nerone, 2001). In the early age of the American press, newspeople used to regard the press as a political stage, but the movement toward market economics had an effect on newspapers, which have since been filled with information on consumer goods (Barnhurst, forthcoming). Gans (2003:23) argues that the shrinking audience has forced the news media to increase their soft news sections to attract, or at least maintain, their share of the audience. This, he adds, has resulted in more jobs for feature writers and fewer for hard-news reporters. American audiences have abandoned the news media, whether print or television, particularly during the 1990s (Gans, 2003:31).

Western news media have thus witnessed an increase of so-called human-interest news. This tendency has existed for several decades, starting with newspapers' introduction of this type of news in weekly supplements, and then as an integral part of the daily editions. This new trend of "service journalism" or "infotainment" (Hjarvard, 1995b; Eide & Knight, 1999; Gans, 1999) includes news on consumer materials and lifestyles. While consumer journalism investigates prices on goods and services to guide readers to the best bargains, lifestyle journalism raises other elusive issues—communication, sex— to guide readers towards a happy and fulfilled life. One of the reasons for the demand for this style of news is the prosperity that readers have enjoyed since the end of the Second World War (Hjarvard, 1995b).

In Britain, politicians have expressed dissatisfaction with the abandonment of daily reporting from the Parliament, but the media have only reacted to the viewers' disinterest in this type of news. CNN, too, relies on health and lifestyle news at the expense of political news (Hodgson, 1999). The boundary between hard news and soft news has become blurred, with the latter becoming a staple of the news diet in the serious (or quality) media, while political news is declining in priority (Hjarvard, 1995b). In fact, this tendency has been a concern of American journalists, who have expressed their concern about reporting news factually while avoiding sensationalism. Despite the decline of pure political news in the American press, American journalists still view their mission from the history of political news reporting; that is, their task is to inform the public, serve as a watchdog, and facilitate democracy.[1] Content analysis of the American press for the last three decades shows that "traditional" stories—government, military, foreign affairs—still occupy the major part of the news, although they have witnessed a decline, while entertainment and celebrity news have increased during the same period.[2] Nonetheless, the subjects of front-page newspaper stories in the United States are still predominantly political, domestic, and foreign affairs, showing only a slight decline during the period from 1977 to 1997.[3]

In his survey of Algerian journalists, Kirat asked the journalists about their own definition of the news; the majority defined it as events "of interest to the nation and people" (1987:168), while others agreed that the news has something to do with the government. In other words, news is politics. This is supported by Bekhait's (1998) study of Egyptian journalists and his examination of news in both national and party press, where he concluded that political news constituted the majority of news, particularly news about Arab politics and presidential activities (or protocol news). Egyptian journalists from both national and party press agreed that protocol news occupies more space than it should in their newspaper, while other "softer" areas—environment, family, human rights, science—should take a more prominent place on the list of news values in the Egyptian press.

Another survey among Egyptian journalists showed that while editors-in-chief agreed that political topics are the most important criterion in their daily reporting, their staff stressed that the news should meet the national interest (Abdel Nabi, 1989).

Turkistani (1989:127ff) identified the news values in the Arabic media based on previous content analyses, which pointed at officialdom as an important attribute of Arab news. Thus, protocol news (or "receive and see-off journalism" as al-Kasim [1999] called it) is an indispensable part of the news diet in several (if not all) Arab countries, and the Arab-Israeli conflict was a major item.

Rugh (1987:7) argues that the politicization of the press was deeply rooted in the Arab press tradition, which made it hard for it to be influenced by the French and British free press tradition, even during the colonial period. This is rather an overstatement. Following their independence, Arab states felt the need to focus on issues of nationalism and pan-Arabism rather than fostering critical journalism on domestic affairs. In addition, there are in fact major differences between the British and French press traditions. While British (and American) journalism is fact-centered, the French tend to mix news and commentary. In fact, Schudson argues that the French and other continental European press did "not develop an objective orientation until many decades after the Americans—and, even then, less fully" (2003:85).

Ayish (2001a) provides two reasons behind the abundance of political news in Arab news media. The first is the political and economic developments in the Middle East during the past fifty years, which have ensured politics a solid place in the news media. The second is the fact that broadcasting was (and still is in several Arab countries) controlled—financially or politically, or both—by national governments. Consequently, news that involves heads of state, or the so-called protocol news, has always been part of the Arabic news. Conversely, the American news media judge the news not by the persons involved but by the newsworthiness of the event at hand (Ayish, 2001a:149f). Ayish (2002b) conducted a content analysis on a sample of newscasts from three Arab satellite channels: Abu Dhabi Satellite Channel, Al Jazeera, and Syrian Satellite Channel. The findings show that the amount of news on pan-Arab and international issues by far outweighs that on local affairs, with the exception of the Syrian channel. Local affairs were almost non-existent on the Al Jazeera and Abu Dhabi Satellite channels, which featured international affairs in 54 percent and 47 percent, respectively, of their news coverage. In addition, human interest and cultural news stories were rather neglected. However, it should also be noted that Al Jazeera, among others, has been introducing cultural and light, short news items, albeit at the very end of the major nightly newscast and accompanied with very short commentary. This in itself, however, marks the channels' interest in this type of news.

The amount of soft news in the Arab press has also been increasing, albeit much later than in the western news media. There is increasing importance given to human-interest news in the so-called pan-Arab newspapers, *Al Hayat* and *Al-Sharq Al-Awsat*. The Lebanese–Saudi *Al Hayat* has regular, weekly supplements directed at different reader segments—young people, business, travel and this type of news is also integrated in the daily paper. Moreover, the press is now regarded as a catalyst for raising public awareness on global issues. For instance, Gulf newspapers have played a decisive role in spreading awareness among young Arabs about the Internet and its effect.[4] Television news, even on the new Arab satellite channels, shows very little human-interest news and focuses instead on political news (Ayish, 2001a). Nevertheless, Arab television news editors admit that their viewers might indeed seek more light news but not at the expense of "informative" news (Turkistani, 1989:252).

Soft news is also subject to seasonal demand, as in Ramadan, when Arab newspapers work on attracting more readers and more advertising revenues by including several "Ramadan quizzes," even competing to offer the easiest one (*Al Sharq Al Awsat*, 7 November 2002).

The priority that the Arab news media assign to political news compared to the declining function that this type of news now has in the western media does not necessarily point to a greater participation of Arab readers in political life in contrast to western readers, who in fact are more occupied than ever with political issues. One qualified explanation for this is the security and prosperity enjoyed by western readers, who no longer fear wars, knowing that wars conducted by NATO do not have the same connotation as did the previous wars their grandfathers witnessed on the European continent. The political stability they now enjoy has directed their fears to other areas, which are not controlled by political consensus but rather unforeseen circumstances. These are issues such as AIDS and global warming (Hodgson, 1999). On the other hand, Arab audiences still live in unstable political conditions, suffering the consequences of long dictatorships and the lack of freedom of speech.[5] Thus, it is not surprising that they not only eagerly consume, but indeed demand, political news.

Interestingly, Jones (2002:172) sees a correlation between political and sexual repression on the one hand and downplaying the entertaining function of the news on the other, such that when authoritarian pressure is lifted, people tend to show a great interest in entertainment news, such as crime, sex, and scandals. In this connection, the degree of tabloidization of the press can be regarded as a measurement of the liberalization of society.

The press's efforts to attract more readers, particular among the younger generations, might indeed be one factor for the increasing amount of soft news. The Qatari newspaper *Ar-raya* for instance, acknowledged that Qatari youth want their newspapers to serve as a forum for pluralistic opinions and contributions (*Al Sharq Al Awsat*, 3 March 2001). In addition, young Lebanese readers declared that they want a mix of news and articles on various aspects of their daily lives: politics, music, sports, and education. They do not buy a certain newspaper because it includes a special supplement for them; rather, they skim all pages of the newspaper to find a story that interests them (*Al Hayat*, 14 October 2003).

According to Ayish's (2002b) study quoted above, the majority of political news items deal with either inter-Arab or international affairs, while news on local affairs is limited and in some media outlets non-existent. In fact, foreign news reporting has received the attention of several Arab scholars due to the general dependency of Arab media on international news agencies as news sources. They see these sources as western-oriented, fulfilling a sort of mobilization function for their governments, although this argument can now be applied only to the print press, due to the limited financial resources available for it to hire its own correspondents. Arab editors acknowledge that they choose to concentrate on foreign news rather than local news because local news is rather boring protocol news (Turkistani, 1989:251f). In addition, the media seem to exercise an agenda-setting function only with regard to foreign affairs (Schudson, 2003:160; Al Haqeel & Melkote, 1995:34).

News Is a Social Responsibility

From a historical perspective, news in the Arab world was not a mass product; rather, its main aim was to provide instruction to officials and governors, guiding them to improve their performance (Ayalon, 1995:15). However, by the middle of the nineteenth century, rulers seemed to spot the powerful role of media. Ismail (1863–1879), the grandson of Mohamed Ali, bought shares in the French paper *Le Temps* to get publicity for his policies and offered generous subsidies to *Al Waqai' al-Misriya* (Ayalon, 1995:19). Thus, news was a sign of modernity, and it flourished according to the role attached to it by the rulers and governors. News media are still seen as a sign of modernization and industrialization of the area. El-Sherif (1980:28) points to the ability of some small emirates in the Gulf to live without an army as long as they can afford their daily newspapers and their radio and TV stations as signs of their economic property and integration in the modern world.

Contemporary scholars point to the power of the news and the social role it plays in a democracy. John Fiske (1987) states that news is knowledge, and since knowledge is power, then news is power. Nevertheless, news has always existed both in democratic societies and under dictatorships. It serves different functions in each society, but it is still regarded as power. The political and social changes that have taken place during the past three decades have motivated analysis of the global changes in the media in new terms.[6] The changes, both at the national and international levels, although apparent in form, are not as obvious in content. In less democratic countries, for example, news media are regarded as powerful tools that should be in the grip of the regime and its supporters. In his examination of news journalism in modern China, Zhao (1998) labels this political rationale as the "party logic," existing side by side with market logic. In the Arab world, despite the absence of full freedom of the press, news has occupied a central role, particularly with the launching of new satellite channels.

Abdel Nabi (1989:24) sees news as "a process through which the reader acquires real knowledge of different events that took place in society during a certain time span." He makes a distinction between events and processes: a train crash is an event, while repairing the rails is a process. Thus, he argues, it is more important to report on the latter since it has a greater role in the public sphere than the former. It is also imperative that news be accurate, factual, and objective. In addition, news has a developmental function in Arab countries, and as such, should add to the reader's knowledge. Abdel Nabi (1989) does not therefore regard crime or protocol news as real news, because it does not add to the reader's knowledge. In addition, learning about the political and social context is a crucial aspect of the news. Mohamed H. Heikal, the former *Al Ahram* editor-in-chief,[7] stated that the reason Arabs do not participate in the public sphere is because they do not know what is going on inside their countries (Abdel Nabi, 1989).

Abu Zeid (2000:32) does not regard Arab media research to have taken into account the special function of news in developing countries. For instance, he said that Egypt adhered to a socialist ideology in the 1960s, yet the socialist definition or characteristics of news were not reflected in the press of the time. Media researchers stress that the moral and social responsibility of newspeople dictates that they should not agitate public opinion, but rather should keep the status quo. It is also important to preserve national unity by not stirring up ethnic or religious conflict[8] (Abdel Nabi, 1989). Likewise, taboo subjects should not be part of the news. Journalists seem to agree with researchers on the importance of developmental news, particularly with respect to preserving the moral and cultural heritage. The majority of Saudi journalists regard the main function of the press as enhancing Islamic values (Tash, 1983:152). The developmental role was also acknowledged by an overwhelming majority of Saudi journalists, while giving the readers what they want was not regarded as a priority (Tash, 1983:152). This view is further endorsed in Kirat's (1987:169) survey, where 65 percent of Algerian journalists agreed that the task of the press is to "help achieve the goals and objectives of development plans." They also agree on the need to bring information quickly to the public, stressing thereby the "reflective" function of the press,[9] while the interpretative task was stressed less (Kirat, 1987:169f). Moreover, journalists from both Arab countries agreed on the importance of using the media to enhance Islamic values.

Around 80 percent of American journalists regard the investigative and interpretive roles of the profession as most important.[10] Investigative reporting can be defined as a serious journalistic practice that seeks to unveil events and processes that are hidden from the public (Aucoin, 2002:209). Political life in the United States during the 1960s and 1970s increased the demand for this kind of reporting, as the Supreme Court reinforced journalists' right to gather information (Aucoin, 2002:215). Nonetheless, the American public is not particularly happy with the watchdog role of the press if it only accentuates political conflict; rather, they prefer investigative reporting that will point at solutions, rather than exposés (Gans, 2003:34). Moreover, investigative reports are basically "morality tales" that seek to preserve moral norms (Gans, 2003:79).

Dajani (1989, 1992) notices an absence of any significant investigative reporting in the Arab press. Arab journalists included in Turkistani's survey (1989:236) renounced investigative journalism as an ideal form, pointing at the difficulty of conducting it in Arab societies. They also pointed toward the entertainment function of the media, particularly broadcasting, as their primary target, rather than burdening their audiences with the "mistakes of anyone, even if it were someone who should be questioned" (Turkistani, 1989:236). Other scholars (Fandy, 2003) reckon that the Arab press has failed in investigative reporting, as journalists are more occupied with writing *maqal* (commentary) than scrutinizing news reports. Needless to say, conducting investigative reporting presumes easy access to information, which is not available to Arab journalists. Algerian journalists, for instance, attribute the failure of the press to foster investigative journalism in Algeria to the lack of protection for journalists and the absence of political institutions to facilitate this type of work (Kirat, 1987:56).

This kind of reporting, however, has been recently introduced by the new players in the Arab media, namely, the tabloids. The Emirates newspaper *Al Bayan*, in its issue on May 5, 2000, argued that Arab readers only seek entertainment and that is why they are attracted to the so-called yellow press. Egypt has witnessed the introduction of a number of newspapers described by the established broadsheets as the yellow press. Among them is *An-naba'*, which pushed the limits of freedom so far as to drive the Supreme Press Council to add a new item on the list of prohibited issues for the press (agitation of religious conflicts) after the tabloid revealed the case of a Coptic monk who was accused of having sex with several women.[11] It may well be that the yellow press took root in Egypt because publishers realized that establishing a daily or weekly tabloid is cheaper than launching a glossy magazine or a private channel. Besides, thanks to a loophole in the press laws, they manage to simply outsmart the authorities and obtain their licenses.

In Jordan, too, several tabloids have been introduced. They differentiate themselves from the established newspapers not only by their content, but also by their investigative reports. George Hawatmeh, then-editor of the *Jordan Times*, said about tabloid papers: "I personally think that the tabloids have had a positive impact. . . .They have courage in exposing or talking about issues that the pro-establishment, the daily newspapers, basically do not tread on. . . . They have investigative reporting, but it is not well-documented, it is not well-researched" (quoted in Jones, 2002:177).

The editor of *Shihan*, a Jordanian tabloid, admits that investigative reporting is not always well documented. The substance, however, is right: a minister has stolen a certain amount; it does not matter if it is 100 or 1,000 pounds; corruption is there. The reason for less documentation is the culture of secrecy among officials in Jordan. It is difficult to get access to precise figures and information (Jones, 2002:179). Thus, such press cannot claim the role of watchdog as practiced in the American press due to the constraints placed on their work.

Arab tabloids are said to be fascinated with moral scandals, particularly sex scandals, and this is one common feature between them and their American counterparts, wherein such scandals are bread and butter. The American press in this matter distinguishes itself from some other western press, for example, in Germany, where such scandals are only a source of laughter but not news (Schudson, 2003:98).

Indeed, the crucial role played by cultural traditions in journalistic practices is what divides journalistic codes in the western context from those applied in Arab countries (Hafez, 2002:241). Some Arab countries, such as Saudi Arabia, explicitly stress the role of tradition in journalistic practices, whereas others do not mention it at all. Journalists are thus not given free rein to write on whatever issue they want, but are constrained by cultural traditions and political considerations. Arab countries can be divided into three categories as far as freedom of speech is concerned. The first category includes the countries whose codes stress freedom as a crucial value: Algeria, Morocco, and Tunisia. The second category encompasses countries where freedom is explicitly limited by other considerations: political, cultural, or religious. Finally, freedom is not at all mentioned in other codes, as in Iraq or the Islamic Media Charter. The efforts of independent journalist associations in western countries to invoke freedom as an essential right, Hafez (2002:33) argues, have resulted in more freedom-oriented practices than in Arab countries, where authoritarian systems impose codes.

Professionally, the Arab Press Union defined social responsibility as the most important consideration for Arab journalists. This was mentioned in the union's charter in 1964, which states that Arab journalists should be honest in expressing their own editorial opinions, bearing in mind the general consequences of those opinions on the general public. They should also be careful in gathering news and should verify the information they have before publishing it. Another obligation is to avoid distorting facts and not to seek personal interests. Journalists are also obligated to protect their sources and not to comment on disorder occurring in other counties unless they have correct information. Social responsibility is not only confined to the task of reporting and commenting on the news; journalists are also obligated to reveal other journalists' violations of these codes (Al Jammal, 2001:66f).

Media scholars agree with this opinion and they even encourage the media to act according to the social responsibility assigned to them. One Saudi professor (Suleiman Ash-Shamry) in communications said that the Arab satellite TV channels carry a great responsibility toward their societies. It is therefore necessary that they confront the United States via the opposition inside the United States, which can support their work. He called for the channels to hold a joint meeting among their boards of directors to discuss the ways they should cover dictatorship or intolerant groups. "We have to work for our own interests in an objective way without agitation," he stressed (Ar-Rayis, 2003:13). When the Iraqi transitional government decided to limit the access of both Al Jazeera and al Arabiya in Iraq, they justified this by the social responsibility of the Arab media to avoid agitating violence, chaos, or cultural and religious conflicts, which these two channels were accused of doing (*Al Wasat*, 6 October 2003:12–13). The same attitude was expressed by the Arab media conference in Kuwait in June 2003 (*Al Sharq Al Awsat*, 11 June 2003).

In contrast to western journalists, Arab journalists usually do not approve of using hidden cameras or the exposure of secret or official documents in investigating official claims. More than 46 percent of Kuwait journalists, for instance, did not approve of methods involving the use of hidden cameras or microphones, and only 40.5 percent approved of the method of claiming to be someone else to get the news (Al Rasheed, 1998:73). Conversely, a survey among United States and foreign journalists in the United States showed that while the U.S. journalists (82 percent of them) were more eager to use "confidential government documents without permission," only 60 percent of foreign journalists in the United States (among them, five were from Egypt, Algeria, Morocco, Kuwait, and Lebanon) approved of this practice or the use of personal documents or photos (Willnat & Weaver, 2003:416).

The belief in investigative reporting in western journalism is perhaps an integral part of the journalists' self-image about their role in a democratic society. This has made journalists define their role as a mix of detective, researcher, and auditor and less as a "communicator" of current news and affairs. An example of this type of journalism was the case of Mark Daly, the BBC journalist who went undercover among police students in the police academy in Manchester, England, where the majority of the population belongs to different ethnic minorities. After the government issued the McPherson report in 1999, which confirmed the feelings of ethnic minorities of being under-protected and over-proportionally suspected by the police, Daly's (and the BBC's) aim was to record and film (with a hidden camera and microphone) racist statements made by police officers and students. Felt forced to act upon the showing of this film, the British Home Secretary promptly sacked six police officers (regardless of whether these six officers were indeed the root of the racism in the police or it was at a higher managerial level). The same British reporter said later in an interview to a Danish magazine that he was involved in another "interesting project" where he and his colleagues would investigate two murder cases to find the "real murderer" (Geard, 2004), a role that is usually claimed by a professional detective or policeman.

Although investigative journalism, as practiced in the United States and Europe, should—at least in theory—contribute to an increasing trust in journalism, the general public in this part of the world express their mistrust of journalists, who are now the least trusted professional group (e.g., in the United States, United Kingdom, and Denmark). This is, argues Onora O'Neill (2002), because the "free" press in the West has unprecedented freedom and power, which sometimes escapes the constraints of accountability demanded in our modern society:

> We may use twenty-first-century communication technologies, but we cherish nineteenth-century views of freedom of the press, paradigmatically those of John Stuart Mill. When Mill wrote, the press in many countries was censored. The wonderful images of a press speaking truth to power and of investigative journalists as tribunes of the people belong to those more dangerous and heroic times. In democracies the image is obsolescent: journalists face little danger (except on overseas assignments) and the press do not risk being closed down. On the contrary, the press has acquired unaccountable power that others cannot match. (92f)

The image of journalists as "auditors" coincides with the view of politics as a form of administration and politicians as leaders whose work can be evaluated. Thus, politics has become administration and journalism auditing (Schudson, 1982:108).

News Is Objective

Developmental progress, together with the increasing literacy rates and urbanization of the readership, all contributed to the notion of objective reporting as a new(s) value. Editors would then regard objective reporting as a means to attract and retain the readers and thereby attract more advertisers (Keeler et al., 2002:46f). During the second half of the twentieth century, American news media debated the ideal of objectivity versus interpretive reporting, and objectivity has been deemed "impossible" to attain (Evensen, 2002:264ff). Arab scholars have shed some light on the role of objectivity in the news reporting in the Arab press, although not all of them adhered to the same western definition of objectivity. Abdel Nabi (1989:80f), for example, concludes his discussion of the role of objectivity in Arab journalism by stressing the role of both readers and journalists. Thus, readers have a natural instinct that helps them distinguish between the false and the true. In addition, the journalists' role is to favor their role in support of the development of their societies over their role as neutral observers. They should seek to guide readers in adopting correct views. To reach this aim, journalists should always critically evaluate their reports and their effect on public opinion (Abdel Nabi, 1989:80f). The vagueness of the definition of objectivity can indeed serve as an "avalanche" for Arab journalists. For instance, the Palestinian Press Law states that journalists will "produce journalistic work in an objective, full and balanced form." However, the interpretation of "objective" reporting is left to the Palestinian Authority to decide, and their strict interpretation of it has caused the closing of newspapers and the detainment of many journalists (Jamal, 2001:274). In addition, the western notion of objectivity as presenting two sides or opinions rather than one is not particularly hailed in the Arab news media, as they might be accused of conspiracy with the enemy, particularly if interviewing Israeli officials. Another source of fear is the interpretation of such interviews as a sign of normalization, a policy that is unsolicited among several Arab leaders and publics alike (Al-Azzawi, 2002). Thus, more than one opinion may not be favorable in this case, as the Arab Press Union advises Arab reporters not to present Israeli opinions, fearing this will only promote Zionist ideologies among Arab audiences (*Azzaman*, 22 October 2003).

Examining journalistic ethics in western and Arab countries, Hafez (2002:229) confirms that truth and objectivity are indeed among the universal media ethics as stressed in the respective ethical codes. Even the Saudi system, based on religious principles, adheres to the quality of truth and objectivity as essential to the news media, confirming previous research (Cooper, 1989, quoted in Hafez, 2002). The following extracts are taken from the ethical code of the Federation of Arab Journalists and apply in Germany, which illustrates this universality (Cooper, 1989, quoted in Hafez, 2002):

> Federation of Arab Journalists:
> "adherence to objective reality and truth"; "correct any published material in case of discovering inaccuracy." § 4
> Germany:
> "respect of the truth and accurate informing of the general public" §1; newspapers and magazines "should also publish views which they do not share themselves." §1/2 (229)

The ethical codes suggested by the Arab Press Union stress the distinction between opinion and news, thus journalists should not wrap their personal opinion in the news reporting structure. It is also not permitted to publish political advertising financed by foreign parties unless it does not collide with national policies (Al Jammal, 2001:68).

Although western journalists agree on the importance of objectivity in news reporting, they do not seem to agree on one clear-cut definition of this notion. One study among Swedish, British, American, German, and Italian journalists has, for example, shed light on the various definitions of objectivity cross-nationally (Patterson, 1998). While Swedish and to some extent German journalists define objectivity as getting to the hard facts, the Italians see it as a means of representing two sides of the story. The latter notion is also adopted by American journalists and to some extent the British, although a great percentage of British journalists also adopt the notion of getting to the hard facts as an important element of objectivity (Patterson, 1998:221ff). Thus, despite the seeming universality of the notion of objectivity, the way it is defined and practiced differs from one culture to another.

Egyptian journalists agreed that their main task is to transmit facts and not to make the news (Abdel Nabi, 1989). In general, they regarded their newspaper's policy to play a crucial role in defining what news is. Readers' interest, however, was at the bottom of the list of factors they regarded as important in defining the news. Also, Bekhait (1998) enforces the same opinion in his survey, which shows that the overwhelming majority of Egyptian journalists regard transmitting information as their main task, while interpreting events did not weigh as heavily. Conversely, the majority of American journalists find it extremely important to scrutinize government claims, underscoring the importance of investigative reporting (Kirat, 1987:212f).

Abdel Nabi (1989) stresses that objectivity is a major characteristic of the news compared to the subjectivity expressed in opinion articles. He referred to the famous Arab historian Ibn Khaldoun, who defined objectivity as the main prerequisite for reporting news (or historical accounts), stressing, more-over, the journalist's responsibility in discerning true from false news. How-ever, objectivity as presenting two opposing opinions is beside the point, assuming that one of the two opinions is misleading or false, because then the media would be helping to promote this opinion.[12] Bekhait (1998) showed that objectivity ranked third on the list of principles journalists claimed to ad-here to when reporting the news. Accuracy was by far the most important fac-tor for the majority of journalists, followed by honesty. Honesty, however, according to Arab scholar Hassan Tawalba (1981, quoted in Al Jammal, 2001:66f), should not necessarily be applied when dealing with the flow of in-formation supplied by international (western) news agencies, which, accord-ing to Arab scholars, are supposed to be loyal to their western governments. Here, journalists have a priority of serving their own national interests, and should not disseminate information that is not verified.

Objectivity is vulnerable to external circumstances. Schudson (2003:187f) defines three circumstances that may jeopardize American journalists' objec-tivity: tragedy, public danger, and threats to national security. In fact, the three conditions might even be present at once, as Schudson illustrates with the events of September 11, 2001, when journalists assumed that "there are no sides" to take (Schudson, 2003:188). Rather, they responded to a collective feeling of solidarity. In fact, Tim Russert from MSNBC expressed just this by saying, "Yes, I am a journalist, but first, I'm an American. Our country is at war with terrorists, and as an American, I support that effort wholeheartedly" (El-Nawawy & Iskandar, 2002b:4). Among American journalists, there is a wish to "re-evaluate" or redefine objectivity and how it works in news reports. CNN reporter Christiane Amanpour once called for this re-evaluation of ob-jectivity, which she thinks must "go hand in hand with morality" (Mindich, 1998:4).

According to Goldie (2003), the American ideal of objectivity is deemed threatened by the new system of "embedded war journalism," where the Pen-tagon instructed 600 journalists from diverse news media outlets around the world and gave them access to the American and British troops. Although there is a historical precedent for the use of such embedding by the Amer-ican military in Vietnam, there are some stark differences in the way it was ap-plied during the recent Gulf War, where the embeds were not allowed to move freely but expected to remain with the units they were assigned to (Goldie, 2003:42). Nevertheless, embedded journalism has generally been seen as pos-itive because it provides a means for journalists to get closer to the soldiers and to report from inside the battlefield, while being vigilant to soldiers' atroc-ities. The disadvantage, though, lies in the compromised objectivity that can result from the close relations with the soldiers. Moreover, Goldie (2003) points out that embedded journalism in Iraq may jeopardize the correspondents' objective reporting due to the troops' control of transportation, so the correspondents only saw what they were allowed to see. Journalists themselves admit that they practice a form of self-censorship lest they loose their embed position (Goldie, 2003.). The cheerleading practiced by some media outlets, such as MSNBC and Fox, was evident during the war,[13] not to mention the wrong information leaked to the press: for example, the report on the fall of Basra on March 23, whereas it first fell into the hands of the allied troops two weeks later (Goldie, 2003:51). During the 1991 Gulf War, the Pentagon sought to prevent journalists from finding out that the smart bombs they used in Iraq were not so smart after all (Gans, 2003:82). Needless to say, not all reports from the battlefield were available to American (and western) audiences; reports on Iraqi casualties, for instance, were rather absent from the reports. Arab journalists, however, embraced the task of this kind of reporting, either as a means of differentiating their reports from their (external) competitors or out of their belief that this is what war is all about. So they relied heavily on reporting on Iraqi civilian casualties and critical reporting of the Americans' practices in Iraq. However, because of these different angles, one can argue that the complete report on the war is that which combined the stories of both sides: the American and the Arab (Khouri, 2003).

The "perspective" that journalists add to their news stories may obscure facts and evidence. For example, Somerville (1999, quoted in Kock, 2002:20) refers to how different "perspectives" adopted by different newspapers affect the final product of the news. As an illustration, he quoted two headlines from the *New York Times* and *Washington Post*, respectively, on June 8, 1995: "Greenspan Sees the Risk of Recession," and "Recession Is Unlikely, Concludes Greenspan."

Editors' and journalists' eagerness to give the floor to the "other party" to ensure their neutrality and objectivity can sometimes be rather embellished. For instance, asking a sample of American newspaper editors whether the letters to the editor they receive show support or condemnation of the recent Iraq war, they admit that the majority were against the war, yet they tried to print as many pro-war letters as possible, lest they be accused of bias (Cunningham, 2003).

Yaghi (1981:69) sees that the *khabar* (news) can hardly be a neutral account of an event, regardless of the freedom given to the news media, because news is part of the media strategy that aims to affect public opinion. In an interview with the editor-in-chief of the Palestinian newspaper *Al Quds Al-Arabi*, he confessed that the news published in his newspaper is 80 percent objective, and yet he describes his newspaper as the most neutral and objective among all Arab newspapers in London (Abu Zeid, 1993:284). Moreover, in his content analysis of several Arab publications, Abu Zeid points to the adherence of some of these publications to certain ideologies, despite their insistence on being the "neutral" medium in the region: for example, *Al Sharq Al-Awsat*'s campaign against the former Egyptian President Sadat until his assassination in 1981 and *Al Hayat*'s support of Saudi policies in spite of the newspaper's neutrality in dealing with other Arab regimes.

Objectivity in the Arabic news media is bound to the attitude of newspeople toward the issue at hand and toward the people involved in it. The Palestinian issue[14] serves as an example of compromised objectivity in the Arab media (Ayish, 2002b:149f). Several, if not all, news media in the Arab countries refer to Palestinians killed by Israelis as "martyrs," while the Israelis are referred to as "aggressors" to keep up the morale of Palestinians in the West Bank and Gaza (Ayish, 2002b:149f). Therefore, politicians and viewers alike were provoked by the appearance of some Israeli officials on Arab news channels and accused the channels of being controlled by the Israelis. One Arab newsman from the Saudi-owned MBC admitted that despite the neutrality his station strived for, they still could not detach themselves from their commitment to pan-Arab issues (Ayish, 2001a).

It is therefore important to consider that news is not and can never be a mere reflection of reality. It is a process of selection and presentation that is subject to the gatekeepers' bias. Or as Schudson puts it, "News is not a mirror of reality. It is representation of the world, and all representations are selective" (2003:33).

Prominence

Previous studies of the news media in the United States revealed that "people were disappearing" from the news, although officials were still the dominant figures as sources and actors in the news media (Barnhurst, forthcoming, chapter two). References to people in terms of gender and social relationship, such as mother or father, were in decline, and instead people are being referred to as members of certain groups—ethnic, national, or professional. One explanation for this is probably a wish to reveal the interaction among social forces in society rather than among individuals (Barnhurst, forthcoming).

In their content analysis of Egyptian news reporting and interviews with Egyptian editors and journalists, Abdel Nabi (1989) and Bekhait (1998) identify "prominence" as one major news value in Egyptian news reporting. Abdel Nabi (1989) concludes that media coverage is confined to presidents, kings, high-ranking officials, or those in the public eye, and says that explains the abundance of protocol news in the Egyptian (and indeed Arab) news media. Politicians are not in the news merely as actors, but also as sources. According to Abdel Nabi's analysis, around 37.59 percent of the news stems from governmental officials, while the newspapers' own staff was the main source of around 29.32 percent of the news. The researcher classified the news into three types, according to source: protocol bulletins, the sources' own press releases, and ordinary citizens (1989:173).

Several Arab media scholars have warned against the press's preoccupation with privileged groups and their neglect of rural areas (Bekhait, 1998; Abdel Nabi, 1989; Abdel Rahman, 1989). Because the elite groups reside mainly in urban areas, news media have been characterized as "an urban phenomenon" that targets these groups and ignores the rural areas where ordinary people live unless a high-ranking official is on a visit (Abu Bakr et al., 1985:34). The party press, on the other hand, uses these areas as a point of departure for their criticism of governmental policies. Although residents in the rural areas of Egypt, for example, represent 70 percent of the population, they occupy only 5 percent of press space (Abdel Rahman, 2002, 40ff).

Rich businessmen are also among the privileged sources of the press. Abdel Nabi (1989) recalls in his interview with one Egyptian editor-in-chief that a bank director happened to phone the editor during the interview to enquire about the "news" or material he sent for publishing. The editor apologized for not publishing it right away, because "the president had just returned from a trip and he would not notice it now," and assured the caller he would wait and print it when the president would be sure to see it (Abdel Nabi, 1989:220). Other research also points to the tendency to include businessmen and portray them as contributing to national development (Abdel Rahman, 2002).

Celebrities have also become a part of the news media diet. Abdel Nabi gives an example of how the accident of a famous Egyptian actress occupied a large amount of space in the newspapers, while a collision between two trains occupied a modest amount of space on the inside pages. The fact that the Arab newspapers (and probably also other news media) are very much dependent on the news provided by international news agencies may contribute to the increasing appearance of ordinary people as actors and sources of information. For instance, the issues of *Al Sharq Al Awsat* on both March 28 and April 3, 2003, depict textually and visually the effect of the Iraq war as seen by ordinary Iraqis. The same tendency was seen in some issues of *Al Arab* and *Al Quds Arabi* during the war,[15] as well as on Arab satellite TV stations, where news programs and documentaries tend to transmit the opinions of ordinary people and not only those of the elite.

Moreover, these prominent figures are not represented equally in the Arab press. Journalists place them in a hierarchal order of the president or king, followed by governmental officials, then celebrities. Ordinary people are, on the other hand, at the bottom of the list. This is confirmed, for example, in the analysis of reported speech. Haeri (2003:104) shows that interviews with the president of Egypt were reported in Modern Standard Arabic (MSA), while other public figures' speeches were reported in a mix of Egyptian dialect and MSA.[16] A comedian or a dancer, however, can be represented in Egyptian dialect, because the sophisticated code of MSA would seem inappropriate (Haeri, 2003:104). Fakhri (1998) has also pointed to this hierarchy of representation using the code of speech. His analysis shows how the Moroccan press represents ordinary workers using Moroccan dialect, while officials are represented with MSA. Thus, access to the news media is not only confined to the powerful—politically, financially, and intellectually—but the code representing them accentuates the gap between them and the less privileged groups.

In fact, those who appear in the media are usually those regarded as a reflection of the genuine image of the nation or at least of the group to which they belong. Abdel Nabi (1989), for instance, points to the abundance of Egyptian news aimed at stressing "national pride" by allocating a great deal of space to remarkable examples of Egyptian citizens who excelled in or contributed to a field, be it art, science, or the humanities. These citizens then serve as a national image or voice to the whole nation, and, accordingly, their achievements are deemed newsworthy and grant them a place in the media. Those who cannot pride themselves on similar achievements are not only less represented but may be pushed aside as violating the "authentic" image of the nation. Thus, a hierarchy is built around those who are deemed worthy to be visible in the local and foreign media as "one of us." For example, a BBC documentary about a poor and less sophisticated Egyptian woman pushed different groups, particularly those from the middle and upper-middle classes, to accuse the program and its team of involvement in a conspiracy against the nation. The poor woman was seen as a reflection of neither the "authentic" Egyptian mother or citizen but merely as a voice that sought to humiliate "the national pride," which is an example of "how criteria of censorship and discrimination are constructed round this cause" (Saad, 1998:405f). The urban, well-educated Egyptians wanted the image of the nation to be confined to historical testimonials as proof of the nation's long civilization or modern edifices as signs of modernity and progress (Saad, 1998:405f). Needless to say, the poor woman's use of vernacular was also seen as a sign of vulgarity in contrast to what users of standard Arabic see as the sophistication of their language.

The Lebanese news magazine *Al Wasat* hammers home the same point in its analysis of the use of images in the news media (*Wasat*, 3 February 2003). The magazine joins those who believe that the images of the less privileged cannot serve as a "true" reflection of the Arab reality, especially images from Iraq and Palestinian areas. Western media tend to show images of poor Palestinians living in dirty quarters, ignoring the images of educated Palestinians such as doctors, who against all odds perform high-quality work under severe conditions. Likewise, images from Iraq, prior to the war, focused on the places that the weapon inspectors visited, ignoring university lecture halls and labs as living proof of scientific progress in Iraq.

To sum up, most images show only negative and not positive aspects of society and do not necessarily reflect reality, which, according to *Al Wasat*, should meet reporters' three most important criteria in news media: emotion, peculiarity, and drama. As an illustration of this, the magazine criticizes that from hundreds of images available from Reuters, the one image used by Arab newspapers to accompany a story on a demonstration of Iraqi women against the American policy toward Iraq was a group of three women who had lost their front teeth (At-Tayiara, 2003:15). Unfortunately the magazine does not point out any specific, possible alternatives to this particular image, but it may have deemed this one image to be unrepresentative since the majority of the protesters presumably had teeth or were otherwise more presentable.

As for news sources, analyses of American news media confirm a tendency to rely on external experts, but those experts are not necessarily there to offer a neutral, qualified opinion, as their choice is motivated by the news organ's own agenda (Schudson, 2003:52). Due to professional constraints, such as deadlines on journalists' work, it is sometimes easy to depend on the available sources rather than seek new ones. Officials and politicians are the available sources, and they in return might use the news media for their advantage, for example by leaking information to undermine a rival (Schudson, 2003:134, 140). American journalists not only report on the news; they have also become expert sources. Newspaper reporters appear on various television programs as experts, and network reporters are treated as experts on the areas they cover. This phenomenon has been increasing over the past half decade, according to previous content analyses (Barnhurst, forthcoming, chapter 2). The same tendency is now seen in Arab satellite television, where prominent press journalists are regularly invited to diverse talk shows, similar to the old print journalist practice of inviting the "celebrities" among media people from television and radio (*Al Wasat*, 5 May 2003:12–13). Also, there is a tendency now among Arab news channels to reflect on their own journalistic practices, inviting news journalists to comment on their work and the difficulties facing them.[17]

Newness

Among the universal news values is newness: that news should deal with a recent event. But immediacy is not an inborn quality of the news. In the beginning of the Arabic press, immediacy did not play such a major role. In Egypt, *Al Waqai' al-Misriya*, said to be the first Arab journal, appeared irregularly, interrupted when the ruler (Mohamed Ali, 1805–1848) was occupied by other matters. The first American newspaper, *Publick Occurrences*, appeared in 1690 (Williams, 2002:3); its timeliness was restrained by geographical boundaries, which meant a delay of months for the news from Europe (Green, 2002:34f). Now, immediacy is an important catalyst in the development of the American press. Thus, Barnhurst (forthcoming) pinpoints the importance of providing rapid information as part of the modern journalistic "scoop" orientation.

Nowadays, immediacy is an important factor in media competitiveness, and it is regarded as one major parameter of *khabar* (news) in the Arab press (Yaghi, 1981:53ff). The media have developed a news commodity that has to be delivered "fresh" every day. Evening editions of newspapers, for example, have been introduced in some Arab countries. In Egypt, Al Ahram, the largest publishing house in the country, has an evening edition of its main product, *Al Ahram*, launched to get a share of the market for evening papers after a competitor introduced the newspaper *Al Misa* (Evening). In Saudi Arabia, Al Jazeera Publishing House, which owns the newspaper *Al Jazeera*, issued the first and only evening newspaper in the kingdom, *Al Masa'iya* (Evening), in 1981. The paper aimed at attracting young readers by increasing the space allocated to their interests. According to the publishing house, *Al Masa'iya* managed to circulate around 30,000 copies daily and their readers came mainly from the Riyadh area. On April 19, 2001, the paper ceased publication as an evening edition and became a morning broadsheet under the name of *Ousra* (Family).[18] On September 11, 2001, *Al Sharq Al Awsat* issued an evening edition to update readers on that important event (*Al Sharq Al Awsat*, 22 January 2003). Kuwaiti dailies distribute their issues later in the afternoon during Ramadan, not in the early morning. Exactly what early distribution means differs from one newspaper to another: *Al Rai Al Am*, for instance, comes immediately after *Iftar* (the end of the daily fast), "in order to keep the reader oriented as early as possible to the important events nationally and internationally," while *Al Anbaa* comes before *Iftar* and in another edition before *Suhur* (the last meal before resuming the fast) (*Al Sharq Al Awsat*, 7 July 2002).

In his analysis of the development of live coverage on European channels, Hjarvard (1995a:337) shows that immediacy is an important factor in the development of news coverage, illustrating this with the 1991 Gulf War, where live coverage was the "ideal" reportage form. In fact, the coverage of this war was regarded by a number of scholars as the breakthrough needed to modernize the Arab media. Thus, new satellite channels appeared, and time allocated to news has increased since then.[19] These channels compete with the old, pro-establishment channels over both the quantity of news offered, and more importantly, its quality. Indeed, live coverage is one competitiveness factor that distinguishes the satellite channels from the old channels; thus their reliance on eyewitness reporting, particularly in times of crises.

The launching of international satellite channels means that viewers now have access to fast and cheap news, literally anytime, which has left newspapers the task of analysis and in-depth reporting (Kock, 2002). Nevertheless, widely circulated newspapers still regard it as imperative to have a network of correspondents, particularly in times of crises. *Al Hayat*, for instance, prides itself on being the only Arab newspaper to have had correspondents reporting directly from the battles of Desert Storm.[20] At least one commentator has recommended that the Arab press regard immediacy as an important factor to get readers' attention if they are to compete with the satellite channels.[21] According to the editor-in-chief of *Al Hayat*, the primary task of the newspaper's correspondents is to gather information first, or to provide the news, and then, if there is time, to provide analysis (Abu Zeid, 1993:399). Thus, news itself is more important than analysis, which is provided in commentaries. One content analysis of *Al Hayat* in 1990 showed that news alone constituted 62 percent of the editorial space, while commentary filled only 11 percent (Abu Zeid, 1993:402).

In sum, it can be argued that there is a form of "value convergence" where news values from western news media affect the traditional values of the Arab media. For example, immediacy is being prioritized now by the Arab media and they have adopted the American tendency to use journalists as experts and sources. This is particularly demonstrated in the news media's reflection on its own work. The emerging genres of political talk shows and debates, conducted in MSA, serve as "visual newspapers" for the well educated, providing them with op-ed sections on the air. Audiences follow the debates to reinforce their existing beliefs about politics and politicians. This role roughly corresponds to the "partisan" role suggested by Blumler and Gurevitch (1995:15), where media personnel serve as editorial guides and politicians as political gladiators rather than information providers. Moreover, the news media in both regions seem to adopt the same principle of objectivity. Although Al Jazeera's slogan is "more than one opinion," there is no clear-cut definition of objectivity, as both Arab and American journalists are aware. Despite the shared news values, there are still a number of differences, particularly in news content. While western news media are reducing the amount of political news items, Arab news media still prioritize political news at the expense of soft news, which is increasing in the western media to attract more viewers. Pan-Arab news media depend on news about foreign policy and inter-relational issues to prove their regional character. Ordinary people are gaining more and more space in the American media, while politicians and officials are still the dominant actors in the Arab media. Nevertheless, the dependence on American news sources, particularly in the Arab press, may well result in the same practice. Finally, American journalists tend to see their mission as exposing the truth about powerful politicians and institutions, whereas this role, rare in Arab news media, is filled by the tabloids. This is illustrated in table 4.1.

Table 4.1   **News Values in American vs. Arab News Media**

Factor	American news values	Arab news values
Content	Human interest at the expense of political news	Political news at the expense of soft news
	Objectivity as a shared value with no clear-cut definition of objectivity	
Time frame	Newness	Newness
Orientation	More local news	Foreign news (with Arab angle)
Function of news	Watchdog role	Social responsibility function
Actors	Politicians	Politicians
	+ Ordinary people	+ Celebrities

Notes

1. National Survey of Journalists, issued by the Committee of Concerned Journalists and the Pew Research Center for the People & the Press. Available online at http://www.journalism.org/resources/research/reports/surveycomment.asp .

2. Traditional news stories dropped from 66 percent in 1977 to 49 percent in 1997, while entertainment news, including lifestyle and crime news, increased from 5 percent in 1977 to 11 percent in 1997. Source: Changing Definitions of News. Produced by Project for Excellence in Journalism, www.journalism.org.

3. Changing Definitions of News.

4. Wheeler (2001) reports on a previous study by al-Khualifi where more than half of the Saudi university students interviewed said that they learned about the Internet from a newspaper or a publication. Kuwaiti newspapers have also followed suit and added Internet supplements/sections.

5. See for example the Freedom House report for 2002.

6. Hjarvard (2001) provides an overview of some of the factors that have affected the international news industry.

7. Heikal was said to be "the most powerful journalist in the world" (Munir,1979).

8. This is particularly important to Egypt, where Christian Copts, despite the absence of reliable statistics, are thought to constitute at least 6 percent of the population. Lebanon, which is rather an exceptional case in the Arab world, is made up of a mosaic of ethnicities and religions (ethnic groups are Arabs 95 percent, Armenians 4 percent and other 1 percent; religious groups are Muslims 70 percent (including Shi'a, Sunni, Druze, Isma'ilite, Alawite, or Nusayri), Christians 30 percent (including Orthodox, Catholics, and Protestants), and Jews. In Iraq, the population comprises Muslims (both Shi'a 60–65 percent, and Sunni 32–37 percent), and Christians and other 3 percent. Iraqi ethnicities are Arab 75–80 percent, Kurdish 15–20 percent, Turkoman, Assyrian, and other 5 percent (CIA The World Factbook, 2003, available online).

9. Mejlby (1999:64f) divides news stories into three types: opinion journalistic, reflective journalistic (merely conveying information from source to readers), and investigative.

10. American Society of Newspaper Editors (1997): The Newspaper Journalists of the 90s. Available online at www.asne.org/kiosk/reports/97reports/journalists90s/coverpage.html.

11. *Al Ahram*, 17 December 2001. This case ended in court, where the editor-in-chief of *An-naba'* was sentenced to three years. *An-naba'* had a circulation of as many as 200,000 copies, and its editorial content focused on scandals and sex crimes. According to Abdel Rahman (2002:73), the 1990s witnessed the introduction of several newspapers that claimed independence and managed to get their licenses from foreign countries. They do not, legally speaking, adhere to the rules of the Supreme Council, but they are subject to the rules of the Ministry of Information (printing laws). Their main source of income is advertising revenue.

12. For trust barometer in Denmark, see Lund et al. (2001), in Britain see O'Neill, 2002, and in the United States see the Poynter report on the 2002 CNN/USA Today/Gallup poll: Al Tompkins. Whom Do We Trust? 24 July 2002. Available at http://poynter.org/content/.

13. This is specifically what the Arab media scholar Abdel Aziz Sharaf said on objectivity, as quoted in Abdel Nabi (1989). Sharaf, according to Abdel Nabi, rejected the definition of objectivity as it is applied in the West, claiming that it has nothing to do with objectivity.

14. See for example "Embedded Reporters: What Are Americans Getting?" by the Project for Excellence in Journalism. Available online at http://www.journalism.org/resources/research/reports/war/embed/default.asp.

15. Arab media refer sometimes to this issue as "the Arab-Israeli conflict" or "problem," thus stressing the involvement of all Arabs in it.

16. Naturally, this assumption needs to be confirmed by quantitative and qualitative analyses of Arab news media output. In fact, this author is currently conducting a quantitative analysis of a two-week sample of pan-Arab newspapers to gauge the effect of "news importation" on the angle adopted in news stories and whether the stories are told from the officials' point of view only or if ordinary people are being represented in the news.

17. For a more detailed discussion on the role of the language in media discourse, see the section on language in chapters six and seven.

18. Al Jazeera, for instance, aired two programs evaluating its work. The first one was *Al Ittijah Al Moua'kis* (The Opposite Direction), aired on 12 December 2000, discussing the need for the channel among Arab news media and inviting media experts and observers to comment on its work. The second one was *Hewar Maftouh* (Open Dialogue), aired on 11 November 2003, marking its seventh anniversary and hosting a number of its prominent journalists and correspondents, including Tayseer Olwani, who was suspected by Spanish authorities of having tight connections to Al Qaeda. The manuscripts of the two programs are available at www.aljazeera.net/programs/op_direction/articles/2000/12/12-12-2.htm and www.aljazeera.net/programs/open_dialog/articles/2003/11/11-6-1.htm.

19. Information retrieved from www.al-jazirah.com, the website of Al Jazeera Publishing House, in October 2003.

20. In fact, the Al Jazeera director said that its competitive coverage forced other channels to extend the space allocated to news programs to 35 percent, up from 10 percent.

21. Abu Zeid (1993:395) quotes the editor-in-chief of *Al Hayat*, Jihad Al Khazin, who prided himself on the number of correspondents his newspaper had during the second Gulf War: two correspondents accompanying the American forces in Saudi Arabia, one correspondent with the American forces in Kuwait, and one on the Turkish-Iraqi border. Al Khazen was sorry that their only correspondent inside Iraq disappeared during the war, which also meant that the newspaper had to depend on international news agencies to cover news from Iraq.

22. Commentary by Al Fahd, *Al Arabi* magazine, 486, 1 May 1999.

II

5

The News Genre

News is not the newsworthy event itself, but rather the "report" or "account" of an event. It is a discourse made into a meaningful "story" in the same way as speech is made up out of elements of language.

—John Hartley, *Understanding the News*

HARTLEY (1982, 2001) ARGUES THAT one should distinguish between the events that make the news (content), from the discourse about that event (code). He defines news not by the event that makes it newsworthy but by the code used to tell about it. The chain of signs that makes an event cannot logically be separated from the analysis of news. It is not arbitrary to choose between signs (like one particular word in the language) without referring to the whole system of signs available to interlocutors. However, focusing only on the code will necessarily reveal only one side of the story. The other side is why a certain topic is newsworthy. In other words, analyzing how the system of signs interacts to produce meaning for news receivers is as important as the analysis of why that particular event should be regarded as newsworthy. To address this issue, it is imperative to understand the social and historical conditions surrounding the news media. A news story is "both news and a story" (Schudson, 2003:177), and therefore analyzing the story should go hand in hand with analyzing the news' referents in the world. Arab and western media scholars alike stress that news stories should answer the questions who, what, where, when, why, and how (Karam, 1992; Fedler et al., 1997). Schudson (2003:190) suggests that "to understand news as culture, however, requires asking what categories of person count as a 'who', what kinds of things pass for facts or 'what', what geography and sense of time is inscribed as 'where' and 'when', and what counts as an explanation of 'why'. Meanwhile, he agrees with John Hartley's claim that news is a textual system, perhaps the most dominant one in modernity (Schudson, 2003:13). Thus, news can be analyzed both as a textual system and as a representational system referring to a certain social reality.

This chapter aims at shedding light on the news genre in the Arab news media. It traces the development of this genre in an attempt to identify a clear definition of news and its major characteristics both as a textual and a social system.

Khabar: The New(s) Genre

The definition of a genre usually follows two schools of language research: some regard it as a product and some as a process (Gledhill, 2002). The generic texts are used as products for various purposes: to describe, explain, instruct. Furthermore, it can be argued that generic texts are also processes aimed at, among other goals,

1. description
2. explanation
3. instruction

Jensen (1986) applies Williams's (1977 in Jensen, 1986) definition of genre in his analysis of the news genre. He points to three main categories in Williams's model: stance of the author, appropriate subject matter, and mode of formal composition (Jensen, 1986:50f). Thus, the stance of the news reflects the journalist's role as an "observer" and the reader's as a receiver of factual information. Jensen points out that the different emphasis on the subject matter in different kinds of newspapers (tabloid versus broadsheets) shows that news is a socially derived communications form. Finally, the composition aspects form the rhetorical link between the sender and the receiver of the news. Consequently, analyzing the news genre should take as a point of departure the news as a product and also as a process bound by social and cultural constraints.

Bell (1991:13) distinguishes between editorial and advertising as the two main genres of the newspaper, assigning the former term to all material that is not advertising. He further divides editorial content into three categories: service information (weather, sports, TV listings), opinion, and news. The third category has several sub-genres: hard, soft, special-topic, with the boundaries becoming gradually more blurred between hard and soft news (Bell, 1991:14).

The development of the news genre in the Arab press was a long, hard process. In his historical review of the Arab press, Ayalon (1995:173) points to the difficulties that faced Arab journalists in the early days. The new medium demanded new genres of writing: clear and understood by a wider audience. However, the journalistic genres sprang naturally from classical Arabic, which had been used primarily in literary genres addressing the small community of intellectuals. News reporting, however, put much pressure on those writers to adapt the Arabic language to the needs of the new medium (Ayalon, 1995; Haeri, 2003). Thus, two genres have evolved: the news genre (*khabar*) and the commentary genre (*maqal* or *maqala*). Still, the newspaper served as a channel for literary writers to publish their work, which they in turn attempted to distinguish from *maqal* by labeling it with new names or genres like diary (*yawmiyyat*) (Ayalon, 1995:182). News reporting, however, was developed by non-literary personalities which, according to several scholars (Haeri, 2003; Abdelfattah, 1990; Parkinson, 1981) had a great effect on its language, which has come closer and closer to the vernacular.

Maqal, on the other hand, is a commentary on various subjects, be they literary, academic, philosophic, or critical. Karam (1992:49) distinguishes among several sub-genres of *maqal*, such as column, editorial, commentary, and diary. Among the major types are the following sub-genres:

1. Editorial (*if-titahiya*) expresses the author's meaning and demonstrates knowledge of the subject and its historical context.
2. Column (*a'moud*) can be either a humorous or serious text whose tone is usually sarcastic, though tending more toward political commentary in modern times.
3. News analysis (*bahth sahfi*) includes long articles explaining important issues (Karam, 1992:47ff).

Arab media scholars and journalists (Fandy, 2003; Hefny, 2003) argue that the new generation of journalists would rather write commentaries than report on news. *Maqal* has become the genre through which writers display their mastery of Modern Standard Arabic and its conventions: choice of classical words, argumentation style, and rhetorical devices. As such, writing *maqal* is the peak of any journalist's career. Some Arab journalists from the Gulf countries, for instance, are said to think of the press as a channel for their commentaries, leaving the task of news reporting to foreign journalists working in their countries (*Al Sharq Al Awsat*, 3 March 2001). *Maqal* is not bound by the same criteria as news reporting. For instance, news should always address a current event, and although this newness is also manifested in commentaries, the *maqal* writer has a freer hand to reflect subjectively on the philosophical or historical issue of his choice.

Contemporary Arab scholars (Karam, 1992; Yaghi, 1981; Abdel Nabi, 1989) still adhere to this distinction between news (*khabar*) and opinion (*maqal*). Karam (1992:33) states that *khabar* is a report on an event or circumstance and that its attributes or values may vary from one newspaper to another. Yaghi (1981:63) points to the necessity of adding background information to the news (*khabar*) so that readers understand the context of the event. He warns, however, about leaving the responsibility of writing background information to novice journalists; this is an important task, he states, that should be confined to the more experienced. Other Arab scholars stress the definition of news as a reflection of real knowledge that has a great effect on the public. For Abu Zeid (2000), *khabar*, in Arabic linguistic terms, is an account that is either false or true. In his opinion, this is a misleading definition, since news has to be true; otherwise, it is simply not news but a fictive account of something that never took place. He criticizes previous attempts to define *khabar*, which he regards as attempts to copy the liberalist definitions with no regard for the cultural differences between Arab and liberal societies. After emphasizing the importance of a new definition of *khabar* that takes into account the situation in the developing world, Abu Zeid (2000:37) defines *khabar* as "an account that describes accurately and objectively an event or idea which affects and meets the interests of the majority of readers while contributing to the development of society."[1] Other scholars stress the developmental aspect of news and its powerful effect in society. Abdel Nabi (1989) sees news as "a process through which the reader acquires real knowledge on different events that took place in the society during a certain time span." Turkistani (1989:7ff) defines news as "any item projecting a real conceived event or a phenomenon that has taken place or will take place and is distributed through a mass medium to be immediately consumed for the purpose of informing or influencing public opinion about that event or phenomenon." Among the main characteristics of news, Karam (1992) points to seriousness. *Khabar*, he says, should also include a detailed account of an event like a salary raise in the public sector, in which case it is not enough to report on the decision of the ministry to increase salaries, but one should give a detailed account of the negotiations that preceded the decision, publishing the whole text of the law, and explaining how the increments have been calculated (Karam, 1992:35ff).

Khabar, according to Karam, is an account of an event or a situation: "The account differs according to the ideology of the newspaper. Major characteristics of news are: seriousness, newness, interest, and simplicity"[2] (1992:33). The news text, then, is not a free account of an event; rather, it seeks to answer the five Ws and the H: Where, Who, When, Why, What, and How (Karam, 1992:44). *Maqal*, on the other hand, is defined as a prose text. It differs from scientific analysis or literary text and it revolves around a current situation or idea.

Notes

1. My translation.
2. My translation.

6

MSA: The Language of News

IN HER AUTOBIOGRAPHY, the Egyptian feminist Leila Ahmed recalled the time she was working in Abu Dhabi and how she encountered young people of Palestinian, Egyptian, Bedouin, and other Arab origins who were taught the culture of literacy in Modern Standard Arabic (MSA). Then she came to realize the local cultural and language differences among Arabs and that MSA was not, in fact, her mother tongue. Her mother tongue was Egyptian Arabic. She finally realized why English and Egyptian Arabic felt closer to her than MSA: they were living languages. In the name of education and Arab unity, the vernaculars and local cultures were being erased, giving way to the written variety of Arabic, MSA. The vernaculars, however, were treated as non-existent not for linguistic reasons, but rather for political ones. Although Ahmed did not argue for the elimination of MSA at schools or as a literary vehicle, she nevertheless called for the "recognition of the enormous linguistic and cultural diversity that make up the Arab world" (Ahmed, 1999:282).

The idea that all Arabs share one language is a misconception. True, they share the written form, but this language is not the mother tongue used in daily communication. The vernacular is the mother tongue, and it varies from one country to another in the forms of Egyptian Arabic, Palestinian Arabic, and Moroccan Arabic, while the written variety is confined to formal writing and speech. The vernaculars are regarded as a menace to the written form; for while the written form claims the unification of Arabs in one language, the vernacular encourages diversity among them. Thus, MSA serves a trans-nationalistic function in the Arab region.

The controversial call-in program, *Al Ittijah Al Mou'akis* (The Opposite Direction), of the Al Jazeera satellite channel, hosted a debate on the written and spoken forms of the Arabic language, discussing the possible death of the written form due to pressure from the vernaculars on the one hand and English and foreign languages on the other. Among the debaters was the Lebanese writer and poet Farouk Rouhana, who preferred to speak his own mother tongue, Lebanese Arabic, arguing that it is an independent language and not just a dialect. The debate raised several important issues, including the effect of English on MSA and the need to reform the teaching of MSA at schools. However, the viewers' contributions revealed generally apathetic attitudes toward language, as one viewer criticized using airtime to debate language instead of using the time to discuss more important (political) issues.[1]

The aim of this chapter is to shed light on the problematic relationship between the vernaculars and MSA, which is also the language of news. As the following overview will reveal, MSA is confined to news reporting and not to other programs, which occupy the largest amount of airtime. The chapter begins with a brief overview of the development of MSA and its emergence as a variety of the classical Arabic of the Koran, then diglossia, or the existence of two variants, one written and one spoken, will be discussed in light of previous research, which in fact points to the existence of triglossia and even quadriglossia. The gap between the written and spoken forms has been the root of many myths about the Arabic language, to wit, its emotivity and its inappropriateness for factual news reporting. The third section of this chapter will briefly review these myths and their counterarguments. Finally, the last section will present the main characteristics of news language in light of its development and the symbiotic relation it has had with foreign languages, particularly English.

The Development of MSA

During the peak of the Islamic empire, classical Arabic—the language of the Koran—was regarded as the only channel for disseminating the Islamic culture

(Haeri, 1997). It was the only language of prestige at that time, which eventually led to the disappearance of other local languages, such as Coptic and Greek (Versteegh, 1997). However, the rulers then felt the urgent need to standardize the language for several reasons, summarized by Versteegh (1997) as follows:

1. The discrepancy between the Bedouin language and other vernaculars in the empire;
2. The desire of the rulers to unite all subjects politically, religiously, and culturally; and
3. The urgent need to standardize the lexicon to ensure uniformity throughout the empire.

Besides being the language of the Koran, classical Arabic was also used in formal prose, such as the sayings of the prophet (Hadith). This secured classical Arabic an exalted position in the minds of Arabs, who saw in it the language of God and spirituality. Nevertheless, this exalted position also meant that the language was, like God, "unattainable" (Fellman, 1973b:28). Holy men and scholars were the only people to have access to it. Thus, it was not a native language handed over from one generation to another, but rather a language that demanded formal education for several years. Moreover, the classical language was confined to the literary genres and concerned certain values detached from modern city life (Fellman, 1973b:29).

Although vernacular Arabic is the daily communication tool for all Arabs, classical Arabic has survived due to its presence in three realms: religion, media, and bureaucracy, of which the first domain plays the greatest role (Haeri, 2003:31). Classical Arabic is thus preserved by daily prayers, whether performed individually at homes or in the mosques, while all other daily activities are performed in the vernacular. Even among Christian Arabs, the Bible and the church services are in classical Arabic. However, Muslims have always considered classical Arabic to be the language of the Word of God. Therefore, Muslims do not expect non-Muslims to master this language, even to the extent of teaching it (Haeri, 2003:49).

Efforts to standardize the classical language resulted in the emergence of MSA as the official language of the Arab counties. The emergence of the Arabic-language newspapers during the nineteenth century was an important contribution to MSA, as the intellectuals who ran those newspapers sought to introduce new terms and syntactic structures to the language (Abdul Aziz, 1986:16). Due to their bilingualism, and sometimes even multilingualism, those western-oriented intellectuals transferred a great number of words and phrases into Arabic (Abdul Aziz, 1986:16). MSA is thus the language of the press, books, and formal correspondence, while classical Arabic is restricted to the religious domain and is performed normally by religious men.

The modernization process in nineteenth-century Egypt, led by the Turkish ruler Mohamed Ali, called for further modernization of the language. In his efforts to improve military education, Mohamed Ali ordered the translation into Arabic of teaching materials, including foreign language books, which could be used for teaching his soldiers (Haeri, 1997:801). This process of translating textbooks has expanded to the present day, resulting in their coming closer to the vernacular. This marked the beginning of improved education possibilities for the masses (Haeri, 1997:801), while simultaneously causing the decline of the role of religious schools, which are based upon teaching the Koran in classical Arabic.

Although MSA is taught in schools, it is treated as a foreign language whose grammar rules are taught in class without practicing the language in real social situations (Fellman, 1973b:30). The students are expected to read literary and religious texts in MSA and to memorize these texts and their grammatical rules without necessarily understanding them (Fellman, 1973b:30). They are not offered, however, classes in conversation in MSA, which makes students connote it with formal and academic purposes (Abdelfattah, 1990:143). For daily communication, the vernacular plays the chief role. This is the language that is handed from one generation to another and is confined to the community in which it is used. Thus, the Egyptian dialect is distinct in pronunciation and grammar from the Jordanian dialect or the Moroccan dialect. This paradoxical situation of having two languages, one for formal purposes and another for informal use, is termed by linguists as diglossia.

Diglossia

Diglossia seems to function as a "mental block" (Ennaji, 2002:79) in the minds of language users because the vernacular, which they practice daily in all sorts of informal communication, is regarded by the state as non-existent. MSA is certified as the official language. This situation means that the vernacular is deemed inappropriate for writing purposes, even if it is merely for exchanging letters. Children, then, develop a block toward their own vernacular, which may lead to schizoglossia (Ennaji, 2002:79). The language users' feelings of separation from their own mother tongue on the one hand, and their detachment from the literary, formal language on the other, forms a "psychological barrier" enforced by the ruling regimes themselves. Even educated Arabs may find it demanding to use MSA in communicative situations where they are much more comfortable using their vernacular. In fact, the educational level of a speaker is not a clear indication of proficiency in MSA. Parkinson (1993) reports on testing the MSA knowledge of educated, urban Egyptians. The test was adopted from the textbooks used in teaching Arabic as a foreign language, and the results showed a gap among the participants according to their educational level. For instance, knowledge of grammar proved high among subjects with a college education related to the Arabic language (Parkinson, 1993:50). Interestingly, however, the same group did not demonstrate high reading or listening skills compared to other groups, which Parkinson justified by their lesser interest in current affairs and thus their reluctance to follow media programs or read the newspapers in MSA. The subjects also expressed a willingness to accept texts with colloquial interferences and without vowel endings (which is a prerequisite in reading MSA) as forms of MSA, which means that, psychologically, MSA is regarded as a mere formalized version of the dialect (Parkinson, 1993:71).

Both Abdelfattah (1990) and Parkinson (1993) point to the lack of adapting MSA to communicative situations in the classroom to guarantee students' proficiency in this language. Abdelfattah (1990:143f) blamed the local governments (at least in Egypt) for ignoring the role of the vernacular instead of encouraging students at schools and universities to apply MSA in real communicative situations and to see the similarities and differences between the written and the spoken languages. This paradoxical situation, of having a language that is never used as the main means of daily communication, yet is exalted and protected beside a vernacular that is officially unrecognized,[2] raises the question of how the written language has come to survive and supersede the vernacular in official status. Haeri (1997) identified one important reason for this: The status of the Koran and the association of classical Arabic with it has ensured the language continuity and prestige up until now. Another factor is the revival of literary traditions since the late nineteenth century, which contributed to the reinforcement of the classical language as the only literary vehicle among Arab scholars and writers (Haeri, 1997:797f; Abdul Aziz, 1986:16). A third factor contributing to preserving the status of MSA is its connotation as the main pillar of Arab nationalism. For example, proponents of the pan-Arabism fostered in Egypt during the 1940s saw in MSA a means for implementing and proving the premises of the ideology (Haeri, 1997:79f).[3] It seemed logical then, that the language that could unite all Arab peoples could not be one of the various vernaculars, but rather the common written language. Classical Arabic has since been seen as a unifying force among Arabs (Haeri, 1997; Rugh, 1987; Fellman, 1973a).

Dividing the language, however, between high and low varieties is a rather simplistic classification. There are several levels between the two (Badawi, 1973). For instance, intellectuals may demonstrate a level incorporating several words from MSA and dialect. Badawi assigns five levels to the Arabic spoken by Egyptians, ranging from classical Arabic to the lowest level of the vernacular. The more educated the person is, the more levels he or she masters. Thus, a university graduate will be able to move among three or more levels, depending on the formality of the speech situation. Moving from a lower level to a higher level is usually related to summarizing the main points in the speaker's arguments, while moving from a higher to a lower level usually happens when the speaker wishes to explain or elaborate on a certain argument (Badawi, 197:206ff). Also, pronunciation of certain phonemes may be used consciously as a means of signaling the speaker's intellectual level, particularly among men. Thus, sociolinguistic studies among Arab speakers confirm men's inclination to mark the classical forms in their oral language more often than women, despite their educational or social background (Haeri, 1997:798). Some linguists describe this situation as triglossia, where the classical language of religion, MSA, and the vernacular all exist side by side. Ennaji and Sadiqi (1994, quoted in Ennaji, 2002:79f) go further to suggest the existence of quadriglossia in Arab countries. This is because a fourth level of language exists and is practiced by well-educated Arabs. This form is called "educated spoken," and this quadriglossia can be described graphically as illustrated in figure 6.1 (Ennaji & Sadiqi, 1994, quoted in Ennaji, 2002:79f).

The link, suggested by Bourdieu (1985), that exists between the upper classes and the official language does not seem to hold in the Arabic-speaking Middle East. There the upper class often adopts foreign languages, while proficiency in MSA is not seen as a sign of high social status. The increasing number of foreign language schools in Egypt means that more and more young people are being drawn away from MSA, whose rigid rules do not appeal to the younger generation. Also, the rise of foreign languages, particularly Eng-

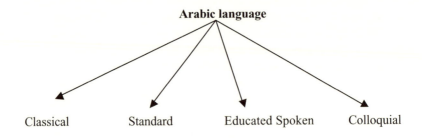

Source: Adapted from Ennaji, 2002.

Figure 6.1   Levels of Arabic

lish, seems to be inevitable in the new economic situation in the Arab region, where the regimes work hard to attract foreign capital and the new job openings demand proficiency in English as a global language. The field study reported in Haeri (1997) reveals that the jobs occupied by upper and upper-middle class people in Egypt demand foreign language proficiency regardless of their knowledge of the official language, MSA (Haeri, 1997:800). Thus, there are two educational systems: a private one where MSA's role is underestimated and a public one of which MSA is an integral part. The labor market further accentuates the gap between the vernacular and MSA: graduates of Al Azhar, the Islamic university, can hardly compete with those who graduated from foreign universities in the same fields. Most of the highly respected jobs do not necessarily demand perfect command of MSA, while low-paid jobs in the public sector necessitate some knowledge of it (Haeri, 1997:804).

At schools, particularly public schools, where classical Arabic should be practiced daily, pupils tend to use the vernacular to answer the teachers' questions (Haeri, 2003:41). In fact, people can no longer see the point of learning the complex grammatical rules of a language whose value lies in its connotation as the language of the holy book and thus as the symbol of Muslim identity across nations. In Egypt, people strive to place their children in private, English-language schools, which pressures public schools to experiment with curricula in English early in primary classes. The increasing enrollment in such private schools has two aims: to acquire a proficient level of the English language and at the same time to escape the "boring" curricula in public schools. Or as an Egyptian mother puts it, "Why should I make my children suffer by learning unnecessary, boring, difficult Arabic grammar when what they really need is sound English? I put my children in an extremely expensive school so that they don't have to endure the pains of studying the ministry's curriculum" (Howeidy, 1999). Hussein and Zughoul (1993:240) note that it is paradoxical that since the independence of the Arab countries from colonialism, English has acquired a more important role in the region's modernization. Furthermore, several university disciplines are taught in foreign languages, particularly English, despite calls for Arabizing the curricula. However, the lack of coordination among Arab academies is among the obstacles to Arabization. Also, the academics' underestimation of MSA as a teaching language and their declining research on Arabization have contributed to the isolation of MSA from Arab universities.[4] The dominance of English, not only as the language of business but also the language of Internet technology, has affected the language used by young Arabs online. One study on the use of Arabic and English by professional Egyptians online, although derived from a small sample, points to a new trend among young Internet users in the Arab region: the use of a Romanized version of the vernacular to chat online (Warchauer et al., 2002).

Myths about MSA

The gap between MSA and the vernacular has made some researchers (Shouby, 1951; Patai, 1973) claim that MSA is incapable of communicating facts, only emotions and repetition. This attitude is close to the classical Sapir-Whorf theory, which connects the negative aspects in a certain language community to the language used in it. Shouby (1951) attributes the "vagueness" of literary Arabic to its rigid structures. This vagueness, he added, could be the immediate result of using certain words without prior, clear definitions, or simply using one word to denote more than one meaning. The rigid character of Arabic grammar is also mentioned as one factor for this vagueness. Shouby concluded that "it has been aptly said that in European languages one has to read in order to understand, while in Arabic one has to understand in order to read." Edward Said (1995, 1978:320f) finds Shouby's arguments rather simplistic, which may point to Shouby's lack of knowledge of how language works. Said relates these augments to the notion of "Orientals" as "mute," while at the same time playing with emotive words for no serious purpose, which he summarizes as follows: "The exaggerated value heaped upon Arabic as a language permits the Orientalist to make the language equivalent to mind, society, history, and nature. For the Orientalist the language speaks the Arab Oriental, not vice versa" (Said, 1995, 1978:320f).

Shouby's arguments stress the emotive nature of the Arabic language and connect this to the impulsiveness of the Arabs as people. This in turn is responsible, according to Shouby, for misunderstandings among Arabs and westerners, because even when the Arab uses a foreign language, he transfers the same impulsiveness to the foreign language. He points to several factors contributing to this emotive character of Arabic, among them over-assertion, over-exaggeration, and musicality of the language. The result is that translation between Arabic and English, for example, proves rather difficult because the meanings expressed in the rather florid Arabic style cannot be rendered with the concrete English words. Said points to the paradoxical situation expressed in Shouby's frequently cited essay: On one hand, the over-assertion of the Arabic language has had a negative effect on the minds of Arabs, while on the other, Arabs can over-embellish their language, which can be described as "poverty combined with excess" (1995, 1978:320f). These myths, related to the Whorfian hypothesis, have long been disproved by cognitive scientists. Pinker (1994:47ff), for instance, provides evidence for his argument that people think not in words but in a language of thought or what he dubbed "mentalese." Thus, deaf people, babies, and animals are still able to communicate in mentalese (Pinker, 1994:47ff).

Abdelfattah (1990:50) states that myths about the Arabic language and its emotivity have in turn accentuated the idea that MSA is inappropriate as a factual language. Arab journalists are claimed to prioritize the rhetorical function of language over the communicative function of transmitting information. They are said to care more about correct phrasing and grammatical rules compared to American journalists, who pay greater attention to facts and statistics (Rugh, 1987:21). This is so to the extent that the news media in countries where Arabic and French are used as languages of daily communication—Algeria, Tunisia, and Morocco—are said to convey ideas that are "part Arab and part French, thereby keeping French perceptions alive in the society" (Rugh, 1987:21). However, one content study of Algerian and Tunisian newspapers in both Arabic and French revealed that the news diet offered in newspapers in both languages was similar (Cooper, 1986). Thus, the concentration of certain themes and topics in the newspapers in French was similar to those exhibited in the Arabic newspapers. The researcher also pointed to the fact that using a foreign language does not necessarily mean that the medium that is using it is different or more elite than the media in the native language; for instance, people in Tunisia could speak French regardless of their educational background (Cooper, 1986).

In addition, the colloquial variety of Arabic is claimed to be more concrete in its meaning, while the classical language exhibits features of vagueness and exaggeration, a problem that is clearly displayed in certain genres, such as editorials, where meaning is hard to "pin down" compared to the concrete meaning in English editorials (Rugh, 1987:22). The disjunction between the vernacular and the classical language is said to be the reason for people's abandoning of the news media in their own countries and resorting to foreign-produced Arabic media like the BBC and Voice of America (Fandy, 2000). However, even the foreign channels use the classical language and not the vernacular; thus, it is not only a matter of code but also content and trust. The question of trust, which Fandy points to, is probably the most important factor in people's attraction to foreign media or to certain channels in particular and is worth studying in detail.

Characteristics of News Language

The introduction of the press in the Arab region resulted in the coverage and description of events for which classical Arabic had no terminology. Since including the vernacular was not considered a viable alternative, classical Arabic was adapted to include terms that previously had been reserved for the private sphere (Ayalon, 1995:173; Haeri, 2003:74). Given that the aim of newspapers is to reach as many readers as possible, the writing had to separate itself from the classical language of literature and adopt a more straightforward style. Early press writers regarded newspapers as just another channel for their literary productions, transmitting the language of literature or *adab* to their political essays. The press was thus "simply another avenue of literary expression" (Ay-alon, 1995:181). The problem lay in the absence of previous examples of using the classical language to report on the mundane. The struggle to create new uses of the written language, and at the same preserve its power, was regarded as a fight between the "'authoritative word and the native word . . . between one's own word and another's word or the alien word" (Haeri, 2003:75).

During the nineteenth century, journalistic language was quite close to the language used in literary genres. Al Azhar graduates were over-represented in the early newspapers, and their formal education had a great effect on the lit-erary style they transferred to their journalistic writings, a matter that was later criticized by editors themselves. For instance, the editor of the Egyptian jour-nal *al-Waqai,* Imam Muhammad 'Abduh, pointed to the unintelligibility of the style used at the time and its failure to serve the purpose for which it was em-ployed (Abdelfattah, 1990:22). However, modernization of the journalistic genres were not particularly welcomed by Arab grammarians, who saw in these emerging genres a threat to the "purity" of the classical language (Abdelfattah, 1990:45f). Some of them went so far as to liken the foreign influence to a "plague that contaminates the language of today" ('al-Samarrai, 1979:101, quoted in Abdelfattah, 1990:45f). Baalabaki (1988, quoted in Hussein & Zughoul, 1993:249) on the other hand argues that journalistic writing has en-riched the Arabic language and has added simplicity and clarity to Arabic style.

Generally speaking, the Arabic journalistic language has been disregarded as unrepresentative of the classical language. For example, Cantarino (1974–1976) disregarded newspapers in his account of the structure of mod-ern Arabic syntax, because, in his view, Arabic journalism is not representative of the literary language (Cantarino, 1974). Additionally, Holes suggests that the Arabic newspaper language has been moving away from the classical liter-ary style and that "today, more than ever, it is in the language of the press, television and radio that external influences on Arabic are most obvious" (1995:255). He suggests that "much of the news reporting in the Arab media is in the form of rapidly produced and often rather literal translations of En-glish or French language news agency reports" (Holes, 1995:256). However, the role of the news media in reaching all social classes should not be under-mined. As Ennaji (1995:97) points out, radio and television in particular are the most popular and powerful media instruments in the region.

The influence of foreign languages on journalistic Arabic is particularly illus-trated with several loan words integrated into MSA. Some foreign words (e.g., folklore, diplomacy) have been adapted to the morphological rules of Arabic (Ennaji, 1995:104f). Titles and technical terms, in particular, are usually trans-ferred unchanged from the foreign languages into Arabic (e.g., doctor, professor, radar) (Ennaji, 1995:104f). Holes (1997:255) supports this claim by pointing to some of the loan phrases in Arab news media as illustrated in table 6.1.

Table 6.1   English Loan Words in the Arabic Press

Shuttle diplomacy	الدبلوماسية المكوكية
Peace process	عملية السلام
The first lady	السيدة الأولى
The lion's share	نصيب الأسد
To give the green light	أعطى الضوء الأخضر
Strategy	استراتيجية
Imperialism	امبريالية
Archives	أرشيف

Likewise, new words are being added all the time to Arabic journalistic jargon. For instance, the increasing access to the Internet in the region has introduced the adjective "Internet"/انترنتي and the adjective "ethnic"/اثنيه despite the existence of the word "ethnic" in Arabic (irqyi').

Ennaji (1995:108) states that foreign words are either translated word-for-word into Arabic (calque) or paraphrased (coinage). The coinage tactic serves three objectives: to avoid the conservative grammarians' criticism of the influence of foreign language on MSA, to live up to the responsibility of protecting MSA as the main national (and regional) language, and to avoid borrowing foreign terms as they are.

Also, it is not unusual to find foreign words transcribed directly into Arabic:

Al Hayat, 18 February 2003:

وزير الداخلية: سنمنع ال"ترانسفير" أيا تكن التكلفة

English translation:
Minister of Interior: We shall forbid the "transfer" whatever it takes.

Here the word "transfer" has been transcribed into Arabic and used in the headline. The quotation marks surrounding the word serve as an indication to the reader that the word is not commonly used. Also, some newspapers transliterate phrases and expressions directly from English, such as "Bush administration" into "ادارة بوش" or "idarit Bush," although the word "ادارة"/"idara" is not normally used in Arabic to refer to a governmental body.

Holes (1997:255) and Abdelfattah (1990) point to some of the loan phrases in Arab news media as illustrated in table 6.1. In addition, Hussein and Zughoul (1993) confirm the frequent occurrence of foreign words in the Jordanian press. They classified the foreign words according to their domains of use and found that the domain of abstract concepts includes the largest number of foreign words, followed by brand names, modern inventions, and automobiles. Terms borrowed from the domains of academia and banking, however, were at the bottom of the list (Hussein & Zughoul, 1993:239).

The use of the vernacular has been primarily confined to one genre, namely *zajal* or satirical poetry, which flourished in the beginning of the twentieth century before it was banned after the First World War (Booth, 1992:424). *Zajal* has always served as a means of communicating political messages in a style less sophisticated than that used in political essays. Among the prominent figures that promoted this kind of poetry was Ya'qub Sannu' (1839–1912) in his satirical journal, *Abu Nazzara Zarqa*, founded in 1877 (Booth, 1992:425). The vernacular enabled the poet to express personal experiences without feeling the restrictions of the classical rules (Booth, 1992:436). This kind of "folkloric journalism" was popular at the end of the nineteenth century in publications such as *'Abu Naddarah* and *'al-Tankit wa 'al-Tabkit* established by Ya'qub Sannu' and 'Abd 'Allah 'al-Nadim (Abdelfattah, 1990:26). Nevertheless, several researchers (Haeri, 2003; Ennaji, 1995; Abdelfattah, 1990; Parkinson, 1981) confirm the influence of the vernacular on Arabic journalistic writing, illustrated particularly by the frequent use of inverted word order in headlines. MSA is indeed a "VSO" language, where verb, subject, and object occur in that order (Eid, 1990:9), while the vernaculars adopt the inverted word order of SVO, or subject, verb, and object (Abdelfattah, 70). Parkinson (1981:28ff) analyzes the frequency of SVO in different genres and shows its overwhelming presence in newspaper headlines and its relative absence from news features on inside pages. Also, serious topics like religion and literature are usually reported in VSO, while light topics like gossip and sports use SVO. Abdelfattah (1990:76) shows that SVO is more frequent in editorials than in straight news and that its occurrence in soft news in 1989 was much higher compared to news from 1935 editions of the *Al Ahram* newspaper. Another study (Ennaji, 1995:98) confirms this tendency, despite the fact that VSO is most common in high classical Arabic.

The current developments in the Arab media and the explosion in the number of satellite TV channels[5] seem to influence the use of MSA. This is due to several factors. First, news and political debate programs conducted in MSA are a competitiveness factor in attracting audiences from the whole Arab world.[6] The use of MSA could be a means of highlighting the pan-Arab character of such programs in the language shared, despite some nuances, by all Arabs, at least passively. Second, TV hosts and media personalities have felt the need to master MSA to participate in the political debates aired by the channels. Even TV speakers and other media types who do not host such debate programs take pride in their knowledge of MSA. Haeri (1997:795) illustrates this with an anecdote mentioned in the Egyptian newspaper *Al Ahram Weekly* about the new media censor who felt the need for a crash course in Arabic to pass the interviews for her job. Despite attending language schools all her life, the new censor had never had a chance to practice or even read much MSA.

The crash course proved fruitful; she managed to impress the program director and she eventually got the job. Third, the pioneer Arab journalists in the nineteenth and twentieth centuries were intellectuals who used the newspapers as channels to express their political opinions. Thus, to mark their intellectual debates, while enticing their readers to adopt their opinions, they had to use MSA because their opinions would be regarded as sarcastic if expressed in dialect. Although the field of journalism has long been open to different types of graduates and undergraduates, the use of MSA still marks the serious character of the news and views expressed in the news media.

The distance separating the vernacular from the MSA as the "authentic" code that is worthy of representing the Arab nation might hinder the complete democratization of the Arab news media. As Haeri (2003b) puts it: "An inclusive and accessible language is essential to freedom of speech. Otherwise, we continue to spin" (Haeri, 2003).

Notes

1. Al Ittijah Al Mouakis, Al Jazeera, aired on 31 August 2001. Available online: www.aljazeera-net/programs/op_direction/articles/2001/8/8-31-1.htm.

2. This is even to the extent that some Arabs still believe that the vernacular is not an independent language with its own grammatical and orthographical rules. They are more inclined to believe that the utterances in vernacular do not comply to any rules, but rather to the speakers' spontaneity. Examples of this attitude were expressed by participants in a live debate about the Arabic language raised on the popular (yet controversial) program *Al Ittijah Al Mu'akis* (The Opposite Direction) on Al Jazeera satellite channel on 31 August, 2001. Transcripts of the program (and other programs) are available on www.aljazeera.net.

3. Suleiman (2003) points, however, to the fact that MSA does not serve as a unification factor in Algeria and Morocco due to the presence of the Berber language; rather, religion carries out that unification role.

4. Syria, however, has pioneered the efforts to Arabize the university curricula, particularly in medical schools (see *Al Arabi*, 1 January 2002).

5. There are more than 100 satellite TV channels, not to mention terrestrial channels, available to Arab audiences (Ayish, 2001:124).

6. The Al Jazeera news director says that the space allocated for news programs has increased from 10 percent to 30 percent of total program time.

7

Values in Language

G IVEN THAT NEWS IS A cultural product, it is then implicit that the act of reading or listening to the news is culturally determined and is not context free. In other words, readers expect a certain structure to the news and certain textual markers or clues that refer to specific references in their social reality. To be able to discern the news genre from other genres (e.g., fiction), readers need to be "news literate" (Hartley, 1982, 2001:5). Moreover, the news structure is not a static entity; it is a structure that differs not only from one cultural context to another, but indeed from one era to another within the same culture.

The prevalent news genres in eighteenth-century United States, for instance, were letters and military communiqués (Vos, 2002:303). News stories were told in chronological order like fiction. Editors filled their newspapers with political essays, which later came to be known as "editorials," particularly after the emergence of the penny press. Then, the commercialization of newspapers allowed printers to hire writers who sent their news (letters) to the newspapers (hence the name "correspondence"). In other words, news became a commodity and was subject to routine production. This era also witnessed the emergence of the inverted pyramid structure (more on this in the following sections), which became the dominant news structure at the beginning of the twentieth century. However, the trend called New Journalism, beginning in the United States in the 1970s, called for the re-introduction of traditional fictional techniques in journalism (Vos, 2002:303).

This chapter will examine the news structure in contemporary Arab news media, especially the print media, in light of previous research. It begins with an overview of the special role of Arab journalists as language custodians, using MSA rather than vernaculars in reporting serious news. The following sections will shed light on the means of reflecting the notion of objectivity textually in news reports. Moreover, the abundance of political news, noted previously, is argued to be mostly reflected in the use of attribution (direct and indirect speech). Also, previous research points to the existence of certain markers that distinguish the objective news genre from subjective genres, such as editorials. Although the vernacular is usually discarded from the news "code," it still appears in the press, especially in "soft" news, to place news subjects and sources in a certain social hierarchy. Finally, the chapter will shed light on how the "newness" of the news is reflected in the use of tense and deictic.

Journalists as Language Custodians

Arab media officials stress the correct use of the classical language and wish to see it replace the vernaculars and take its place as the main tool of daily communication among Arabs. The code of journalistic ethics approved by the Council of Arab Information Ministries addressed this matter, calling for Arab journalists to act as guardians of the classical language and the literary heritage of the Arab nation (Hafez, 2002:242; Al Jammal, 2001:69). In her analysis of Moroccan newscasts, Ennaji (1995:108) found that the use of vernacular words in the hard news is rare (less than 1 percent), which she justified by the need for more prestigious and formal language in the news media. Yet, apart from newscasts and religious programs, media output is in vernaculars. Haeri (2003:33) counted the number of programs in vernacular and classical Arabic on the Egyptian Channel One. Her findings show clearly the use of vernacular in 85 percent of airtime. Newspapers, however, use the classical language, reserving the vernacular for humorous or sarcastic commentaries and caricatures. Yet, vernaculars have played a crucial role as the tool of interpersonal communications among peoples. This is why politicians "sprinkle their rhetoric with colloquial phrases" to connect with their listeners (Rugh, 1987:22). Gamal Abdel Nasser, for instance, used to begin his speeches to the nation in classical Arabic and then shift into colloquial Egyptian (Holes, 1993:37). The media's role was to convert these vernacular phrases into classical Arabic when reporting on the speech. Thus, the printed version of the speech (or the version reported in the TV news bulletin) tended to exclude this "localized flavor" (Rugh, 1987:22) because the president "is not supposed to utter a word in the vernacular" (Haeri, 2003:104). Thus, language marks the difference in social hierarchy and authority in society and at the same time emphasizes the news media's role in upholding this difference and guarding classical Arabic from the impurity of the vernacular.

The short deadlines that rule journalistic practice have forced editors and journalists to depend on the quick translation of incoming news from international news agencies and sources, paving the way for the introduction of new terms and expressions in the MSA used in the news (Abdelfattah, 1990:42f). The foreign influence is not confined to the borrowing of lexical terms but also syntactic structures from Turkish, French, English, Spanish, and Persian, among others (Abdelfattah, 1990:42f). This foreign influence in journalism is regarded by some grammarians as more harmful to the language than the vernacular (Abdelfattah, 1990:46). Arab academies have joined this critique, and in their 1988 conference the problem was extensively debated. The outcome was a set of recommendations to hire more language correctors in the news media, besides strengthening the Arabic language curriculum offered in journalism departments (Abdelfattah, 1990:46). The Arab Academy in Cairo still accuses the media of damaging MSA in an attempt to promote the vernaculars, ignoring that a vernacular is only understood within a country's borders and not shared by all Arabs. As a consequence, the academy fears that the bonds with MSA would be eventually broken.[1] The academy has further called for politicians and media people to use the Arabic language properly as a means of mobilizing and unifying the Arab peoples. Since entertainment still occupies the largest share of media content, the academy recommended that Arab ministries of information increase the airtime allocated for songs in MSA to counterbalance the large amount of time devoted to vernacular songs.[2] On the other hand, advocators of the modernization of MSA defend the development of the language used in news media and regard it as a contribution to journalistic work (Abdelfattah, 1990:44).

To ensure the classical language variety used in the newspapers, correctors join the editorial staff, and they are also accepted as members of the press associations (Haeri, 2003:61). Their task is to maintain the authenticity of the classical language in reflecting "the Arab character," a task that cannot be accomplished by using the vernacular, since it is only "local" (Haeri, 2003:64). Although Arab newspapers usually rely on correctors, there are some stylistic differences among newspapers in the different Arab countries (e.g., spelling of foreign names, titles) as a consequence of the lack of clearly defined stylebooks shared among these newspapers (Abdelfattah, 1990:19). The increasing number of journalists with no background in the literary genres was what the press needed to provide news reporting in a less sophisticated style. Language researchers point to the increasing use of vernacular syntactical structures in the press. This has meant, however, that the press language differs from country to country, just as do the vernaculars. One previous corpus linguistic study showed that there were indeed differences in the lexical choice between Egyptian and Lebanese newspapers (Parkinson & Ibrahim, 1999). The editor-in-chief of *Al Hayat* said once that his newspaper sought to recruit journalists from all over the Arab world and that he wanted his newspaper to be a forum for writers from the Maghrib countries (Tunisia, Morocco, and Algeria), but that the reports sent by the journalists from these countries sometimes needed translation because of their style, as well as the use of archaic and unintelligible words (Abu Zeid, 1993:374f).

The news media have thus played a role in the modernization of the language. Television plays an important role as a medium even for illiterates, but television sets are not yet available in certain rural areas, where radio is still the medium of necessity. Newspapers and print media play a role among literates and intellectual readers, but it is argued that the newspaper information may be transmitted to illiterates orally (Abdul Aziz, 1986:15). Booth (1992:423) argues that the actual circulation of newspapers is in fact greater than the paid circulation, since there is a tradition of reading the newspaper content aloud to friends and families. This is why the print media "played a role that was out of all proportion in the political and cultural life of the country, when the literacy rate was still very low" (Afaf Lutif al-Sayyid Marsot, quoted in Booth, 1992:423).

Objectivity in the News Narrative

A news story is a narrative, which includes setting, characters, and themes. The defining difference between news narrative and fiction is that the former deals with real events and people. Having said that, it is important to remember that the two forms of narrative share the same code: language. The previous chapters point to the bias connected with several journalistic processes—selection of news, choice of sources, embedded journalism—that can be called non-linguistic. On the other hand, examining the selection of words and tenses, the use of direct or indirect speech, the news lead, and the structure of the news story reveals linguistic biases.

Previous research on the news genre, especially television news, points to the presence of two important dimensions that form a typology for understanding media genres: the degrees of objectivity and emotionality (Berger, 1992, quoted in McQuail, 2002:334f). High objectivity and weak emotionality will usually be indicative of actuality genres (news), while low objectivity and strong emotionality are characteristic of drama, for example.

George Orwell was probably the first to explore the vagueness of news language in his seminal 1946 essay "Politics and the English Language." He refers to the notion of "euphemism" or the use of vague, undefined expressions to conceal the mental picture associated with certain phenomena. For instance, "elimination of unreliable elements" can be used to refer to imprisoning people without a fair trial. Likewise, there are a number of words available for journalists to use in a news story about poor people, for instance: poor, impoverished, underprivileged, and destitute (Geis, 1987:15). Words are usually associated with certain connotations; what some linguists term "presupposition." To avoid presuppositions in the readers' minds, the writer should use precise words devoid of any ambiguity. However, as Geis (1987:16) points out, this is not applicable in the world of journalism, for the simple reason that journalists address the whole community, the more knowledgeable as well as the less knowledgeable. Thus, journalists are obliged to use ordinary language, regardless of its mental presuppositions, and "as a result, since there is often no value-free vocabulary for reporting on events, reporting will, in such cases, inevitably not be value-free" (Geis, 1987:16). Tuchman (1972:664ff) defined some of the journalistic strategies to maintain objectivity to include reference to facts, presentation of two conflicting opinions, use of supportive evidence, use of quotation marks, and the structure of the story itself in an inverted pyramid style, beginning with the most important information of the story. Even the division of the newspaper itself, with the (hard) political news in the first pages and the soft news in the inside and back pages, is another sign of this objectivity (Tuchman, 1972:671).

Arab scholars agree that objectivity is important to news reporting. Karam (1992:151ff) gives an example of how to report objectively: if a journalist has to report on a conflict between policemen and a group of students, it is important to read the statement of the police, that of the students, and students' unions' and witnesses' statements to be able to report on all points of view. He states, however, that it is difficult to be wholeheartedly objective in news reporting, because journalists' ideologies or beliefs may interfere.

Arab scholars argue that objectivity or "objectifying devices" are marked in both the form and content of news stories. In form, the so-called inverted pyramid structure is used for serious, political news. In content, adverbs are avoided and, instead, certain initial markers are used, distinguishing news stories from subjective genres. In addition, the passive voice is generally avoided in short political news.

Structure

One main characteristic of objective reporting is the inverted pyramid structure. This is to say that the news report begins with the most important information and moves downwards toward the least important (Bell, 1991:168f). Thus, the narrative of a news story differs greatly from that of literary and film narratives, where events can be reported chronologically until the climax is reached toward the end of the narrative. A typical news story, however, gives the editor the chance of trimming it from the end; therefore, the least important details are kept to the end paragraphs. This is because a news story is never an individual work but rather a group work. Thus, a reporter sends a report on a certain event, then a journalist will write a news story about the event, and the sub-editors and editors will check and re-edit or reorder the story before they send it to printing (Bell, 1991:32ff). The inverted pyramid style is regarded as one of the pillars of objectivity in news reporting, together with the ethic of representing both sides of the story, relying on facts, non-partisanship, and balance (Mindich, 1998:8). Objective reporting was seen to mark the end of the partisan press and the beginning of the so-called penny press in the United States (Schudson, 1978).

Abu Zeid (2000:151ff) defines the inverted pyramid (*haram maqloub*) as consisting of two parts: the top of the pyramid, summarizing the main event and its consequences, and the body of the pyramid, presenting the details in descending order, beginning with the most important and ending with the least important. This structure is illustrated in figure 7.1.

This form is also more convenient for the busy reader who does not have time to read through the whole article, since it will be enough to skim quickly

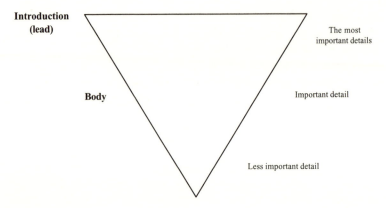

Figure 7.1   Inverted Pyramid Structure

through the first two paragraphs to get an idea of what it is about. Thus, the opening paragraphs gain tremendous importance since they should, in principle, provide the key information about the news, answering the basic questions of who did what, where, when, why and, not least, how. The following paragraphs will then elaborate on the introductory paragraphs and more details will unfold slowly throughout the rest of the news story. An alternative to the "inverted pyramid" style is the "upright pyramid," which is characteristic of the dramatic style most often encountered in literature. Here, the writer begins with the details and goes slowly toward the climax of events. Here the reader is urged to carefully read through all lines of the text to grasp the meaning of the story.

Moreover, reporters can choose not only between the inverted pyramid and upright pyramid structure, but they can also mix both structures in what is called the "step pyramid" or ziggurat, as illustrated in figure 7.2.

Abdelfattah's study (1990) on the language of the Egyptian daily *Al Ahram* from 1938 to 1988 shows that the structure of the news text has indeed undergone a radical change from complex to more simple and universal. The inverted pyramid structure was first introduced in the Egyptian press in the 1950s by the founders of the Egyptian daily, *Akhbar Al Youm*. Before that date, journalists used to adopt a rather chronological reporting of events to "keep their readers in suspense" (Abdelfattah, 1990:17). The founders of *Akhbar Al Youm* were particularly influenced by American journalistic traditions and tried to transfer some features of the American style to their newly established newspaper (Abdelfattah, 1990:17).

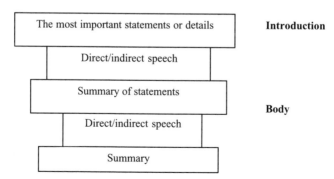

Figure 7.2   Step Pyramid Structure

The following is an example of the inverted pyramid structure:

Al Rai Al Am, October 1, 2003

واشنطن: اعتقال العمودي بتهمة تلقي أموال من ليبيا وزيارته لها

أعلن مصدر قضائي ليل الاثنين ـ الثلاثاء، ان عبد الرحمن العمودي، الذي يعد من اهم اعضاء الجالية المسلمة الاميركية،... اعتقل الاحد بتهمة قبول اموال من ليبيا وزيارته لها.

ومثل العمودي، ....، امام محكمة الكسندريا (فرجينيا) اول من امس، بعد يوم من اعتقاله في مطار دالس الدولي في واشنطن بعد عودته من رحلة طويلة في الخارج.

وكانت الامم المتحدة رفعت في 12 سبتمبر العقوبات التي فرضت على ليبيا في 1988 بعد اعتداء لوكربي عام 1988 الذي اوقع 270 قتيلا، لكن واشنطن ابقت على عقوبات اقرتها من جانب واحد في عهد رونالد ريغان، العام 1986، ردا على عمليات ارهابية في روما وفيينا، اتهمت طرابلس بلعب دور فيها.

English translation:
Washington: Al Ammoudi detained after accusation of receiving money from Libya

A judicial source said yesterday that Abdel Rahman Al Ammoudi, who is one of the important members in the Muslim community in the United States...was detained last Sunday after being accused of visiting and being financed by Libya. Al Ammoudi... was brought before the Alexandria Court (Virginia) the day before yesterday.... On September 12, the UN increased the sanctions against Libya, which have been in effect since the Lockerbie attack in 1988... but Washington chose to resume the sanctions that were decided upon during the Reagan presidency in 1986 as a reaction to terrorist attacks in Rome and Vienna, in which Libya was accused of involvement.

The news report begins with a lead sentence that summarizes the whole report. Then more details are provided as the story unfolds.

In his content analysis of selected editions of *Al Hayat* in 1990, Abu Zeid (1993:396ff) points to the reporters' extensive use of the inverted pyramid structure in news stories (56 percent of all news) and the mixed structure (23 percent), which he uses as a proof of the newspaper's objectivity and the journalists' mastery of the journalistic genre. Also, the inverted pyramid structure was extensively used in news reports (66 percent), more than the upright pyramid structure (24 percent). This was interpreted as a means of marking the newspaper's reliance on news rather than views.

News versus Views

Khalil (2000:164) argues that the news text in Arabic is distinguished syntactically from the views text. The distinction is rather subtle, and it lies in the absence of certain initial markers in the views texts and their extensive presence in "hard" news texts. These initial markers appear less frequently in editorials as compared to news texts. Editorials are characterized by the frequent occurrence of nominal structures in the initial position (Khalil, 2000:230). The initial markers serve as indicators of the news reports' factuality and detachment, and their absence emphasizes the subjective nature of a text (Khalil, 2000:231). Examples of such markers follow:

Al Sharq Al Awsat, November 1, 2003

ومن جهة ثانية دعا السناتور.... الرئيس بوش الى التحدث للشعب الاميركي، واطلاعه على حقائق الوضع في العراق، وما تواجهه الولايات المتحدة من مصاعب وتحديات.

English translation:
On the other hand, the senator . . . called for President Bush to address the American people and present the facts about the situation in Iraq, and both the difficulties and challenges which face the United States there.

Al Rai Al Am, October 1, 2003

الى ذلك أكد مدير اللجنة الوطنية لشؤون الاسرى والمفقودين ربيع العدساني لـ «الرأي العام» تحويل اللجنة لـ 28 ملفا لاسرى الشهداء الى مكتب الشهيد ...

English translation:
About this, the director of the National Committee for Hostage Affairs, Rabi'a Al Adsani, stressed to Al Rai Al Am that the committee transferred 28 cases concerning dead hostages to the martyr office . . . .

Such markers may also include phrases such as "it is worth mentioning/*al jadiir bith'thikr/youthkaru*," which introduce background information:

Al Sharq Al Awsat, November 1, 2003

يذكر ان الرئيس بوش الذي عاد الى البيت الابيض من اجازة شهر امضى معظمها في مزرعته في تكساس، سيواجه فور استئناف نشاطه غدا الثلاثاء، ثلاث قضايا رئيسية هي: الوضع في العراق، وجهود السلام في الشرق الأوسط والتي على وشك الانهيار، والوضع الاقتصادي الذي تواجهه الولايات المتحدة.

English translation:
It is worth mentioning that President Bush, who returns to the White House after a month's holiday at his ranch in Texas, will face three important issues when he resumes his activities tomorrow: the situation in Iraq, the failing peace efforts in the Middle East, and the economic situation of the United States.

Ennaji (1995:102) points to the occurrence of such prepositional phrases in the initial positions to foreground certain events or items.

Avoiding the passive voice:

Another characteristic of objective news reporting is the use of the active voice instead of the passive voice. Arabic news is usually reported in the active voice. Abdelfattah (1990:62ff) states that one of the reasons for this is that Arabic news reports are usually written with no voweling and thus the use of the passive voice may add to the ambiguity of the sentences. He quotes the following example from *Al Sharq Al Awsat*, where the distinction between the words "*musta'mirin*" (colonizers) and "*must'marin*" (colonized) is ambiguous due to their identical written form in the absence of voweling:[3]

إن استغلال المستعمِرين للمستعمَرين لمن دواعي الأسف

English translation:
The exploitation of the colonized by the colonizers is regrettable.

The passive voice, on the other hand, is usually used when reporting on accidents and is used particularly in connection with verbs such as "killed/*qutila* or injured/*u'siba*:"

Al Sharq Al Awsat, May 2, 2003

قتل رجل أمن أردني وأصيب أربعة آخرون أمس في مطار الملكة عليا الدولي في العاصمة الأردنية عمان جراء انفجار قذيفة كانت في حقيبة صحافي ياباني... وأخضع الصحافي الذي لم يكشف النقاب عن اسمه للاستجواب....

English translation:
Yesterday, a Jordanian security man was killed and four others were injured at the Queen Aliya Internal Airport in Amman following the explosion of a bomb found in a Japanese journalist's case. The journalist was questioned and his identity was not revealed. . . .

Alternatively, the journalist might insert the name of the newspaper as the recipient of news:

Al Rai Al Am, October 1, 2003

محمد بن مبارك لـ «الرأي العام»: الديموقراطية ليست وباء نخشاه
علاوي لـ «الرأي العام»: قريبون من صدام كشفوا عن اختلال وضعه العقلي
أبو الحسن لـ «الرأي العام»: الإساءة للإسلام لن تحدث في عهدي

English translation:
Mohammed Bin Moubarak to Al Rai Al Am: Democracy is not a disease, which
we should fear
Alawi to Al Rai Al Am: Sources close to Saddam revealed that he was on the verge
of insanity
Abu Al Hasan to Al Rai Al Am: Offending Islam is not going to happen during
my period in office

There are several syntactical means used to avoid the passive voice, such as
the use of nominalization by inserting "*tamma*" followed by the verbal noun
(Adbelfattah, 1990:64):

Al Sharq Al Awsat, November 1, 2003

واوضحت ان من بين الأجانب الذين تم تسليمهم لسفارات بلادهم 8 اتراك و3 روس، وفتاة أوكرانية، وأخرى اوزبكية، و4
نيجيريين ...

English translation:
And it explained that among the foreigners who were returned to their embassies
there were eight Turks, three Russians, one Azerbaijani, four Nigerians . . .

Abdelfattah (1990:92ff) showed that the use of *tamma* followed by the
verbal noun was indeed over-represented in the 1989 sampling of *Al*
Ahram compared to the 1935 sampling, where the full passive was preferred.

The use of an indirect agent immediately after the adverbial "*bi*"/by,
"*biwasitat,*" or "*min qibal*" is another syntactical means used to avoid the passive voice. A previous study of Arabic newscasts (Ennaji, 1995:101f) found
that the active voice dominated (almost 86 percent of all simple sentences)
and that when the passive was used, the agent phrases "*bi,*" "*biwasitat,*" or "*min*
qibal" were preferred. Some linguists regard the use of this adverbial structure
as an example of a direct influence of foreign languages on modern Arab
journalism (Abdelfattah, 1990:89).

Another alternative is adding an impersonal subject instead of the real subject:

هزت ستة انفجارات عنيفة وسط بغداد

English translation:
Six strong explosions shook Baghdad

Al Hayat, April 30, 2003

شهد الخط الأخضر الفاصل بين شطري جزيرة قبرص ضغطا هائلا من جانب القبارصة الراغبين في عبوره...

English translation:
The green line dividing the island of Cyprus witnessed a tremendous pressure from Cypriots who were eager to cross it . . .

Attribution

The abundance of political news in the Arab media means that politicians and officials serve as news sources. Thus, one would expect that the news would include long quotations from politicians expressing opinions on issues or parts of a president's speech. Because news reporting is supposed to reflect the impartiality and credibility of the news media, reported speech is utilized as a means of contributing to this image (Waugh, 1995:129). Previous research on Arabic journalistic discourse has indicated that the importance of quoting a source lies in the reporters' wishes to add authenticity to their news reports (Al-Shabbab & Swales, 1986). Citations are thus another means of displaying the news institution's objectivity by presenting the opinions or statements uttered by one or several parties on a certain issue.

While officials constitute the main sources quoted in political news items, CEOs and managers may be over-represented in economic and business news items, especially since various newspapers have regular business supplements concerning Arab and international companies. In addition, cultural news items might depend on various public figures, like actors and artists, as sources. Reports on accidents, tragedies, and the like may also depend on direct speech to add the personal dimension needed for the news item and to make it easier for readers to identify with the persons involved.

The use of direct speech is as common in western news media as it is in Arab news media. For instance, (hard) political news usually includes citations from more than one source:

International Herald Tribune, June 18, 2003[4]
"This is a positive step on the part of France, and we are expecting France to treat these people as dangerous terrorists," said the Foreign Ministry spokesman, Hamid Reza Asefi, according to a statement quoted by the official press agency IRNA.

Al Sharq Al Awsat, June 5, 2001

قالت صحيفة أمس إن شركة «سوني» عملاقة الإلكترونيات، تعتزم دمج مراكز عملياتها المالية الأربعة في طوكيو ونيويورك ولندن وسنغافورة في مركز واحد يكون مقره لندن

English translation:
Yesterday's paper said that Sony, the electronics giant, intended to merge the four centers of its financial operations in Tokyo, New York, London, and Singapore into one center to be based in London.

Reporting speech using the verb *qala* (said) indicates a mere reiteration of what the source said. There are other verbs, however, which can be used in reporting speech that normally carry an interpretative meaning: for example *awdaha* (explained) or *shaddada ala* (stressed). Other verbs, such as *adafa* (added), can be used as a stylistic device to ease the flow of discourse:

Al Sharq Al Awsat February 24, 2003

وقال: "إننا لا نمانع في تطبيق قرار مجلس الأمن رقم 1441". ...وأضاف انه من الصعب تقدير الفترة الزمنية للحرب المحتملة على العراق...

English translation:
He said: "We do not object to executing the Security Council Decision no. 1441" ... and he added that it would be difficult to estimate the time frame of the expected war on Iraq.

There are in fact various ways of reporting speech in news texts. One way is to insert the exact wording of the quoted party surrounded by quotation marks and followed or preceded by the verb "says." Another way is to report it indirectly, by using the phrase "said that" before the quoted speech; in this case, quotation marks are needed. A third way is to use participles such as *qa'ilan* (saying), as illustrated in table 7.1.

In his analysis of the language used in the *Al Ahram* newspaper in 1935 compared to 1985, Abdelfattah (1990:135) showed that active participles as verb substitutes occurred more frequently in the 1935 samples than in the 1985 samples. He attributes that to the influence of literary styles on Arab journalistic genres in the 1930s. In the 1985 samples, on the other hand, the tendency was to produce long and complex sentences—hence the decrease in active participles—and to replace active participles with relative clauses and *tamma*-type structures (Abdelfattah, 1990:109f & 135).

Table 7.1   Use of Participles in Arabic News

He commented on that by saying that . . .	وعلق على هذا قائلا
And he pointed at . . . adding that . . .	وأشار إلى أن... مضيفا أن...

Although there is abundance of examples of the use of direct speech in Arabic news texts, there is also an overwhelming number of examples of indirect speech using verbs such as say, add, state, or declare. These verbs occur typically in political news where the actor or speaker is a high-ranking official, such as the president:

Al Sharq Al Awsat February 24, 2003

...لكنه اعترف أن الوقت متأخر جدا في محاولة الوصول إلى هذا الحل...

وطالب الشيخ محمد الدول الكبرى بالتصرف حسب مقتضيات الشرعية الدولية...

واستبعد الشيخ محمد تكرار النموذج الأفغاني في العراق...

وأشاد ولي عهد دبي بالموقفين الألماني والفرنسي...

وسخر الشيخ محمد من فكرة رسم خريطة جديدة للمنطقة بعد الحرب المحتملة على العراق.

...لكنه أعرب عن خشيته من احتمال تعرض العراق لمخاطر التقسيم...

واعتبر الشيخ محمد تراجع الاهتمام بالقضية الفلسطينية بأنه تراجع مؤقت...

English translation:
. . . but he admitted that the time is now late for reaching that solution . . .
and Sheikh Mohamed called for the big countries to act according to the international legislation . . .
and Sheikh Mohamed discarded the repetition of the Afghani experience in Iraq . . .
and the Crown Prince of Dubai praised both the German and French views . . .
and Sheikh Mohamed ridiculed the idea of drawing a new map of the region after the expected war on Iraq.
. . . but he expressed his concern of the risk of dividing Iraq . . .
and Sheikh Mohamed considered that the current indifference toward the Palestinian case is rather temporary.

The choice of which verb to add to indirect or direct speech does not seem to be arbitrary. For instance, verbs such as *zada* or *adafa* (added) can be used as variants of *qala* (said), as they mainly add to the flow of the text. However, verbs such as *shaddada* or *akkada ala* (stressed that) occur in more empathic contexts, where they help to add reliability to the reported speech and cast off doubt as to its invalidity. Furthermore, the use of these verbs is subject to the reporters' interpretations. It is highly unlikely that the quoted party explicitly said "now I highlight" or "now I stress." It is usually not recommended in American journalism to use verbs such as hope, feel, or think (Fedler et al., 1997) because they carry the journalist's interpretation of what the source said rather than reporting what was said.

Although previous research (Khalil, 2000) points out that Arabic short news items rarely use adverbs, the above verbs carry the meaning of adverbs. For instance, the verb *sakhira* will be rendered as "said sarcastically" in English.

Cole and Shaw (1974) show that the use of "powerful" verbs (contend, insist, argue) for "to say," though more vivid, make the story less believable for the reader.[5] The use of attributive verbs is claimed to be a form of journalistic bias. In fact, Merrill (1965) defined six categories of bias: attributive, adjectival, adverbial, contextual, outright opinion, and photographic.

Al-Shabbab and Swales (1986) examine the use of attribution in the Arabic and English news of the BBC and Syrian Radio. They show that the BBC's Arabic service used to include a large number of attribution features, not so much quoting officials in the Middle East but quoting two other sources: their correspondents and the news itself or *al'anbaa' tufiid* (the news says). This is justified by the desire to maintain objectivity and impartiality (Al-Shabbab & Swales, 1986:38).

Al Rai Al Am, October 1, 2003

وكشفت مصادر حضرت الاجتماع، ان ... وقالت لـ «الرأي العام» ان مطالب الصحافيين «تركزت على ضرورة الحد من زيادة الرقابة في سورية في الوقت الذي يزداد فيه الانفتاح الاعلامي في العالم ....

English translation:
A well-connected source that attended the meeting revealed that . . . and said to Al Rai Al Am that the journalists' appeals focused on the need to lessen the Syrian censorship, especially now that media around the world enjoy increasing openness . . .

Khalil (2000:235) states that Arabic short news usually begins with the source of the news report, be it an official or an institution.

Al Rai Al Am, October 1, 2003

طلبت لجنة الخارجية والأمن البرلمانية من رئيس الحكومة الإسرائيلي اريبل شارون، اتخاذ قرار نهائي بشأن صفقة تبادل الأسرى مع «حزب الله» من دون ان يعرض الأمر على اللجنة.
وأعلنت مصادر سياسية وأمنية، وجود ازمة تعيق اتمام صفقة تبادل الاسرى ...
وذكرت المصادر الاسرائيلية، انه يستبعد اتمام الصفقة قريبا كما تم الاعلان خلال الاسابيع الماضية بسبب تعثر المفاوضات

English translation:
The Foreign Affairs and Security Committee requested that Israeli Prime Minister Ariel Sharon take a final decision about the hostage exchange deal with Hezbollah without submitting the case before the committee.
Political and security sources declared that there was a crisis, which hindered the deal. . . . The Israeli sources said that it was unlikely that the deal would be completed soon, as was announced several weeks ago, due to the failing negotiations.

The journalism textbook of Fedler et al. (1997) identifies some of the uses of attribution as giving evidence for a statement or connecting a controversial opinion to its source. The use of attribution in the Arab news media seems to serve these purposes. Besides, the abundance of political news has given politicians and other formal sources the opportunity to appear too often in the news, both as sources and actors. Finally, the tendency of Arab journalists to begin with the source of news has also contributed to the increasing use of attribution.

Hierarchy of Textual Representation

The hierarchical representation of individuals and groups in the news media is not only confined to the Arab media. Abdelfattah recalled the stormy news report in the *Washington Post* on July 1, 1990, when the mayor of Washington was quoted verbatim commenting on Jesse Jackson's running for mayor: "I'm gonna be like that lion the Romans had. They just keep throwin' stuff at me, you know? But I'll be kickin' their asses, every time!" (1990:64f). This quotation offended the black community, which accused the newspaper of being racist. The mayor himself protested later, accusing the newspaper of using this quotation on purpose to ridicule him and show him as non-intellectual.

In her analysis of the language of Moroccan news, Ennaji (1995:109) shows that a more sophisticated form of the Moroccan dialect was used by interviewees in radio and television news, and that the interviewees adhered to a strategy of mixing the vernacular with MSA due to their inability to express their thoughts fluently in MSA. Ennaji (1995) provides four reasons for code mixing in the news:

1. to influence the audience's attitude in a certain debate;
2. to involve ordinary people in the debates, adding realism;
3. to signal dependence on various news sources; and,
4. to personalize the news.

Examples of articles where hierarchy of speech is represented are found in cultural news about celebrities, ordinary people's problems, and women's issues. The following is an example from *Al Hayat*, February 24, 2003, dealing with the increasing divorce rate in Egypt and the dramatic increase in the price of wedding parties, which is a major problem facing many couples:

وقفت الأم العجوز في شرفة منزلها، في ضاحية شبرا المكتظة بالسكان، تترقب مواكب الأفراح خصوصا في عيد الأضحى...فهي تمضي غالبية وقتها في الشرفة، تتحسر على الماضي وتكتشف جديدا في الحاضر. ووسعت نظرها لعلها تلحظ أزمة مرور حادة أو عراكا بين سيارة أجرة وأخرى خاصة، ومحاولات تهدئة من المارة. "يا إخواننا إحنا في عيد وفى السيارة عروسه عيب كده". لكنها لم تلحظ كثافة العراك كما في العام الماضي. انتظرت اليوم الأول ثم الثاني فالثالث فالرابع من دون جدوى، وسألت نفسها. "إيه اللي حصل للناس بطلت تفرح ولا إيه، بقى في العيد أشوف 15 موكب بس! ياااه. كنت أشوف 40 و 50 موكب إيه اللي حصل السنا دى".

English translation:
The elderly woman stood on her terrace in the crowded Shoubra [a quarter in Cairo] *watching the wedding parades, especially during the Adha Eid* [Muslim feast]. *She spent most of her time on the terrace, lamenting the good old days and discovering new causes for complaint in the present. She always looked carefully in the hope that she would see how the parades would cause a traffic jam, and how car drivers would quarrel with one another and the passengers would interfere in the disputes among the drivers, saying, "Let us not quarrel during Eid; we have a bride sitting in the car." But the woman did not witness as many quarrels as there were last year. She waited for it to happen; she waited the first Eid day, then the second, then the third, then the fourth, but nothing happened. She asked herself, "What happened to people? Did they stop getting married or what? I only saw fifteen parades during Eid! Oh... I used to see forty and fifty parades. What happened this year?"*

The journalist begins with the scene of an old mother standing on her terrace watching wedding parades. It is like drama, where a narrator is inserted to tell the reader what is happening in the text. The reader gets into the mind of that woman (real or not) and finds out what she yearns to see in the street: a wedding parade. The old woman's speech was transcribed as if she uttered it in vernacular, with no editing by the journalist, whose presence is marked by MSA.

Several Arab newspapers still depend on foreign news services as primary sources. *Al Sharq Al Awsat*, for one, subscribes to a number of American news services, which allows it to reproduce articles from American publications. This implies that the importation of ready-made news will necessarily include new structures and genres, which might diverge from the traditional news genre in Arabic. The following is an example of a (hard) news story printed in *Al Sharq Al Awsat* on September 1, 2003, after permission from the *Washington Post*. The article takes the form of the story of an Iraqi family that faced death because they were in the wrong place at the wrong time:

قصة أسرة وجدت نفسها وسط تفجير النجف.. علي أراد مصافحة الحكيم فقتل.. وشقيقه تخلف لقراءة القرآن فنجا
النجف: دانيال وليامز * قال علي عباس انه كان يريد أن يصافح يد محمد باقر الحكيم الذي ألقى خطبة الجمعة بمسجد الإمام
علي. التفت علي عباس، وهو عامل عمره 20 سنة، إلى اقربائه الذين جاءوا معه من العمارة، على بعد 175 ميلا إلى الشرق،
لزيارة الضريح، وقال لهم انه يريد، قبل المغادرة، أن يودع آية الله محمد باقر الحكيم، الذي كان قد ألقى خطبة مؤثرة. وكان
عباس يريد أن يقول انه يلتقي الحكيم شخصيا.
*خدمة «واشنطن بوست» ـ خاص بـ«الشرق الأوسط»

English translation:
The story of a family that found itself in the midst of an Al Najaf explosion: Ali was killed before he could shake hands with Al Hakim ...and his brother was rescued as he went out to attend the Quran reading.

Al Najaf. Daniel Williams*
Ali Abbas said that he wanted to shake hands with Mohammed Baqir Al Hamik,
who conducted the Friday service at the Imam Ali mosque. Ali Abbas, a 20-year-
old worker, came with his relatives from their home, which lies 175 miles to the
east, in order to visit the holy shrine. He told them that he wanted to say goodbye
to Al Hakim, whose preaching was powerful. Abbas wanted to meet Al Hakim
personally....
* Washington Post Service

The news story not only deviates from the traditional genre rules of the inverted pyramid structure but also from the rule of including formal sources
and actors. Here, the main actors are ordinary Iraqi people. It should be
stressed, however, that quantitative analyses are needed to confirm the effect
of this convergence between traditional Arab and foreign (American) genres,
both with regard to structure and to actors and sources in the news.

Newness: Tense and Deictic

It is rare that newspaper readers have any interest in yesterday's newspaper; it
is more common to read today's "fresh" news. News then is a product with a
short life cycle. That is perhaps why Benedict Anderson (1983) called it a
"one-day best-seller." The structure of news is said to reflect this timeliness by
beginning with a headline and a lead presenting the most important (and recent) events, while temporal references to past (background) events will usually be included in subsequent paragraphs. The temporal organization of the
news story may be arranged in different times by referring to a specific date,
using time adverbials to connect events, or deictic anchored in the present as
a reference point (Bell, 1991:201).

The present tense prevails in the headlines of both the American and Arab
press:

International Herald Tribune, April 25, 2003 (Brinkley, 2003):
U.S. Tells Iran to Stay out of Iraq
Authority Is up for Grabs in Baghdad

The choice of present tense, in particular, adds immediacy to the event
being reported on. The tense used in Arabic headlines is in most cases the
present tense, as illustrated in the following example:

Al Hayat May 20, 2003

واشنطن تطرح مشروعاً معدلاً لا يحدد مدة إحتلال العراق

English translation:
Washington Proposes Plan Amendments That Do Not Specify the Time Frame for Iraq Occupation

Al Hayat, April 30, 2003

بوش يبدأ احتفالات النصر بلقاء مع الجالية العراقية

English translation:
Bush Commences Victory Celebrations with a Meeting with the Iraqi Community

One reason for using the present tense is to make the events appear actual, thus showing the reader that the newspaper is reporting about events that have just happened. Another reason is that the present tense normally dramatizes the event, making it sound as if it is currently happening. Also, the present tense de-historizes the event in question, meaning that the event does not seem to belong to a particular time; on the contrary, it is detached somehow from the past. As Ennaji (1995:99f) argues, the present tense as used particularly in headlines and lead paragraphs adds vividness to news reports, while body texts and commentaries are usually reported in the past tense. The use of the past, she continues, is one main feature of the narrative style of news reports.

Newness is then reflected in two dimensions: in terms of time, the news story should report on a current event, and in terms of style, the present tense may be utilized to convey newness (Karam, 1992:33ff). However, the use of the present tense is usually confined to the headlines. The news texts are usually written in the past tense and they include adverbs marking that tense. For example, a quantitative study on time references in five Lebanese newspapers shows an abundance of adverbials; indeed, forty-four news texts of the forty-nine on the front pages of these newspapers had adverbs such as *ams, awal ams, sabah ams* (yesterday, the day before yesterday). On the other hand, only one text refers to *sabah al yaum* (this morning), and two refer to the future: *al osbo'a al qadim* (next week) ((Karam, 1992:33ff). Geis (1987:148) argues that the sense of immediacy can be conveyed by other means than the use of the present tense. The use of certain deictic expressions, such as today, here, or this, anchor the news story in the proximate time frame. However, such deictic expressions are more common in the electronic media than in the press.

Ekecrantz (2001) argues that news is not just anchored in the present, devoid of history or future. Rather, future temporal references prevail, especially in the English-language press, as news usually refers to speech acts (promise, forecast), for example, as in the following headlines from the *Financial Times*: "Europe to Discuss 40,000-Troop Rapid Deployment Force"; "Fed to Decide Today."

Ekecrantz (2001) argues that temporal references may differ from one culture to another. Whether time is anchored in the past, present, or future in the Arab news media is a matter for further investigation.

Notes

1. From a news item available on www.aljazeera.net on 19 March 2001.

2. From a news item available on www.aljazeera.net on 2 April 2001.

3. Ennaji also shows that the news bulletin in Moroccan broadcasting, for example, rarely marked case endings. The majority of the case endings, however, were found in the headlines (1995:100).

4. Elaine Sciolino, France arrests 150 Iranian dissidents, *International Herald tribune*, 18 June 2003.

5. Cole and Shaw (1974) conducted an experiment to see if the use of attributive verbs other than "said" and body language statements (e.g., "gesturing his left hand, he contended that . . ."). They showed three versions of news stories to a number of subjects, where the first version was the original story with "said," the second version had an active attributive verb (e.g., contend, insist, etc.), and the third version included a more active attribute verb and a body language statement. The findings showed that version one stories were judged as the most believable and accurate, while version two ranked in the middle, and version three was the least believable, although the most exciting.

Conclusion

THE INFORMATION REVOLUTION THAT CHARACTERIZES the Arab media scene at the moment has not been confined to the news media alone. New genres have been introduced, gaining vast popularity among regional audiences. Reality television, for instance, has been imported by the Arab channel MBC via a program called "al-hawa sawa," while *Who Wants to be Millionaire* is still the audience's favorite program, ensuring its Lebanese host, George Kerdahi, wide popularity. Other genres which were never part of Arab television culture, for example exorcism in the MBC program *az-Zil* (Shadow), have also appeared.

As this book argues, there is a news value convergence among Arab and American news media, fostering new values such as newness and live reports, the extensive use of experts, analysts, and news journalists themselves as sources, and the western notion of objectivity, both in form (two sides of the story) and content (textually). News media have been undergoing unremitting development since the 1991 Gulf War, when CNN and the BBC were Arabs' eyes on the war. Now, Al Jazeera, Al Arabiya, and Abu Dhabi, among other channels, are competing with the foreign channels in covering wars and crises in the area, offering the Arab version of the story. Regional competition among Arab channels has resulted in an abundance of political talk shows, which supplement the op-ed articles in the print media (Gans, 2003:29). In fact, one Saudi media scholar says that time and globalization will contribute to modernizing Arab journalism even more, now that the Arab news media have adopted the slogan "more than one opinion," fostering the new journalistic practice of investigative journalism. Nonetheless, an analysis among Lebanese journalists showed that censorship is still regarded as a main obstacle to freedom of speech in the Arab region. According to those journalists, political pressures and the little effect the press has on public opinion in the region foster censorship and control (*Al Watan*, 10 April 2003).

However, news media outlets cannot be regarded as a substitute for genuine political institutions and catalysts for democratization in the region. True, they have succeeded in introducing new genres and have claimed an agenda-setting function, but this is confined to foreign policy issues. The belief that these media alone are exactly what is needed for Arabs to join the democratic and free nations (see for example al-Kasim, 1999) is an overstatement when the current change has not been accompanied by genuine political change or by the establishment of political institutions to ensure citizens' participation in political life. Although the commercialization of the media is one important catalyst for such change_as happened in the United States_the Arab middle classes are still drawn to the entertainment sector, while the news media target the intellectual elites. Moreover, informed citizens do not alone constitute what it takes to produce democracy, which is better served in countries with functioning economies and secure middle classes (Gans, 2003:59f). Arguing that informing citizens is enough to ensure political participation is wishful thinking. While the more informed people are, the more likely they are to participate politically, this participation is subject to other factors like income and education, as Gans (2003:57) points out. Thus, it is important to remember that news is by no means a substitute for broader general knowledge.

The Arab road to democratization, however, does not necessarily follow western theories and experiences, simply because of the different political realities in the two spheres. Also, the effect of globalization can neither be exaggerated nor interpreted in western-based theories, such as deterritorialization (see for example Sakr, 2001). Zhao (1998) argues that the commercialization of the Chinese press during the 1990s, the emergence of popular tabloids, and mixed ownership forms have all created a new situation that can hardly be described in terms of existing (western) theories. In fact, Zhao chooses to refer to this new system as a "propaganda/commercial model." Likewise, Abdel Rahman (1986, quoted in Ayish, 2001b:126) suggests a theory of dependence to describe Arab media systems, arguing that news media are likely to depend on foreign sources as long as the media drifts away from domestic affairs. This theory emerged in Latin America in the 1960s and 1970s, and among its adherents was the Egyptian scholar Samir Amin. According to his theory, the developed nations enjoy too much dominance of the developing nations to allow the latter to form independent policies. Instead, the developed world sets the standards and exercises control over the developing countries, which remain dependent.

One the one hand, the higher literacy rate and increasing number of youth in the region, together with external media competition, may have helped introduce changes that are mostly symbolic: new genres and news formats. External pressure will also continue to play a decisive role, for internal pressure alone might prove too weak to enforce political and social changes (Rothstein, 1995:79f). On the other hand, the media's indulgence in covering foreign policy issues at the expense of internal and social affairs further limits their effect toward democratization. The competition among the new satellite channels has pushed them to arrange more daring political talk shows, but these normally deal with other countries' issues rather than internal issues. Indeed, Fandy (2000) calls this phenomenon "anywhere but here," referring to the fact if Egyptians want to know about Egypt, they are better off watching Al Jazeera, while a Qatari is better served by reading Arab newspapers from outside Qatar to keep informed of what is happening inside Qatar. A Qatari citizen summarizes this problem by saying that his "information about what's going on outside Qatar is much stronger than all the information of what's happening inside" (El Nawawy & Iskandar, 2002a:85). Moreover, entertainment still constitutes the majority of programming available on Arab satellite channels, and the cultural and political broadcasts still target the intellectual elites, as one Arab scholar argues in a recent dissertation on the performance of these channels.[1] Alterman (2002) observes that censorship is no longer a viable issue in Arab information strategy, and that governments can now be held accountable for their policies in the new environment of transparency. This is rather wishful thinking, for as long as foreign policy issues occupy the largest space in the news media, neither transparency nor accountability is secured.

On the bright side, the satellite channels have managed to spread a sense of competition among all channels, terrestrial or satellite, for the benefit of the audience. While satellite channels focus mainly on foreign policy issues, terrestrial channels have managed to focus to a certain extent on internal affairs, particularly social issues, which were regarded as taboo in the past. For instance, Egyptian television airs a live program dealing with sensitive issues such as female mutilation, unemployment, *urfi* marriage (informal marriage), dual citizenship, and intermarriage with Israelis (Elbendary, 2001). And unless satellite and terrestrial channels address local issues, preferably in the vernacular, the debate will remain only partly democratized because foreign affairs direct the attention of audiences away from their internal problems, which are left to dramatizations, for "fiction writers can avoid intrusiveness of power by claiming that the work is fictional and any correspondence to reality is a mere accident" (Fandy, 2000:393).

Also, several Arab tabloids and party press, as well as national talk shows, might indeed have the largest effect on future development. The watchdog role adopted by Arab tabloids and party press might serve a twofold purpose: increase attention to the news and its role at the national level, while revealing the deficiencies of the current regimes. Governments and officials certainly react, even violently, by imposing strict penalties upon such publications, but as Gans argues, "when a large proportion of the citizenry wants to hear the watchdog's message, totalitarian regimes become fearful of losing the complete control they believe they need to stay in power" (2003:82). Tabloids and national programs do what the new pan-Arab media do not do: debate local issues (preferably in the vernacular), and thereby secure the widest response locally.

The new trends in the Arab news media will be unlikely to create a new (Habermasian) public sphere, where Arab publics interact with no fear of censorship and freely criticize their political institutions. This, however, does not rule out that there exists a feeling of common identity among Arabs congregating around the new media. Schudson (2003:69) points to Anderson's (1983) concept of "imagined community" to better account for the interaction among news audiences, where the public interacts as a group around common issues, be they social or political. This community shares one image of itself and its nation. There is evidence for the existence of this type of connection among Arabs now, such as in the pride in seeing the news—particularly from the recent Iraq war—through Arab eyes; in having alternatives to foreign news sources; in feeling that the controversial coverage of their news media has somehow turned the tables and it is now the West (United States) that is provoked by its image in the Arab media; in learning more about the policies, albeit foreign policies, of other Arab countries; in being more and more familiarized of other vernaculars and lifestyles; in feeling that they are being taken seriously as informed audiences. Paradoxically, the emergence of the new communications channels has served two seemingly contradictory functions. On the one hand, the entertainment and cultural programs pull Arab audiences to accept cultural and national diversity by watching drama, music videos, and programs produced in vernaculars other than the culturally dominant dialect (i.e., the Cairo dialect). On the other hand, the news media pull in the other direction by using one linguistic code (MSA) to (re-)ascertain the role of formal language as an ingredient of Arab nationalism.

Still, credit is due the Arab new media, which have pushed the limits of freedom and enforced a healthy competitive spirit among media outlets, fostering new journalistic practices. At the beginning of the book, I quoted an old Arab adage that says, "Journalism is a profession that hunts out trouble." The new generation of Arab journalists is living up to this saying. As one journalist from Al Jazeera commented, "What we do at Al Jazeera puts us in lots of trouble" (El-Nawawy & Iskandar, 2002b:5).

Note

1. The thesis is reported on at www.aljazeera.net/cases_analysis/2003/8/8-24-1.htm.

References

Abboud, Nazir. 1984. *Newspaper language. Ibrahim al yazigy* (in Arabic). Beirut: Dar Maroun Abboud.

Abdel, Nabi, and Abdel Fattah. 1989. *Sociology of news* (in Arabic). Cairo: Al Arabi Books.

Abdel Rahman, Awatef. 1989. *Studies in Egyptian and Arab press: Current issues* (in Arabic). Cairo: Al Arabi.

___ 1991. Arab world. In Nordenstreng, Kaarle, and Michael Traber (eds.), *Promotion of educational materials for communication studies.* Report of Phase I of UNESCO/ IPDC Interregional Project by IAMCR/AIERI. www.uta.fi/textbooks/index. html (accessed 15 June 2003).

___ 2002. *Issues of the Arab region on the press in the 20th century* (in Arabic). Cairo: Al Arabi Press.

Abdelaziz, Salah Ahmed. 1981. *The coverage of international news in ten American and Arabian dailies: A comparative analysis.* Unpublished masters thesis, Ohio University.

Abdelfattah, Nabil M. S. 1990. *Linguistic changes in journalistic language in Egypt, 1935–1989: A quantitative and comparative analysis.* Unpublished doctoral dissertation, University of Texas at Austin.

Abderrahmane, Azzi. 1989. The Arab press: An evaluation of William Rugh's typology (in Arabic). *Al fikr al-arabi* 58:169–183.

___ 1998. *Mass media in the Grand Maghrib: Morocco—Algeria—Tunisia.* Department of Communication, IIU: Malaysia. www.geocities.com/Athens/Ithaca/8257/ maghrib.htm (accessed 18 October 2003).

Abdul Aziz, Mohamed. 1986. Factors in the development of modern Arabic usage. *International Journal of the Sociology of Language* 62:11–24.

Abu Bakr, Yahya. 1980. Towards an intra-cultural news exchange in the Arab states. In Alcino, Louis da Costa et al. (eds.), *News values and principles of cross-cultural communication,* 16–26. Paris: UNESCO.

Abu Bakr, Yahya et al. 1985. *Development of communication in the Arab states— Needs and priorities.* Paris: UNESCO.

Abu Khadra, Faisal. 2002. Wanted: Arab investment in Western media. *Al Sharq Al Awsat,* 9 October.

___ 2000. *The art of news reporting* (in Arabic), 4th ed. Cairo: Alam Al Kotub.

Abu-lughod, Ibrahim. 1962. International news in the Arabic press: A comparative content analysis. *Public Opinion Quarterly* 26 (4): 600–612.

Abu Zeid, Farouk. 1993. *Arab émigré press* (in Arabic). Cairo: Alam Al Kotub.

Adwan, Abdel Jabbar. 2003. Scandalous media search for satisfaction. *Al Sharq Al Awsat,* 27 March.

Ahmed, Leila. 1999. *A border passage: From Cairo to America: A women's journey.* New York: Farrar, Straus and Giroux.

Al Abd, Atef. 1995. *Studies in Oman media,* Vol. I–IV (in Arabic). Cairo: Dar Al Fikr Al Arabi.

Al Assad meets with Syrian journalists. 2003. *Al Hayat,* 2 October.

Al-Azzawi, Jasim. 2002. Should we talk to the enemy? *Transnational Broadcasting Studies* 9.

Al Dhaheri, Amina. 2000. The image of women in Arab media. In *Women's rights and the Arab media,* a report by the Center for Media Freedom. Middle East & North Africa: CMF MEENA.

Al Haqeel, Abdallah S., and Srinivas R. Melkote. 1995. International agenda-setting effects of Saudi Arabian media: A case study. *Gazette: The International Journal for Communications Studies* 55:17–37.

Al Imam, Ghassan. 2002. Commentary. *Al Sharq Al Awsat,* 21 May.

Al Jammal, Rasem M. 1990. Foreign news in Arab newspapers (in Arabic). *Al Mustaqbal Al Arabi* 135 (13).

Al Kadry, Nahound, and Souad Harb. 2002. *Female and male journalists in television* (in Arabic). Beirut: Arab Cultural Center & Lebanese Women Researchers.

al-Kasim, Faisal. 1999. *Crossfire:* The Arab version. Freedom of the press in the Arab world. *The Harvard International Journal of Press Politics* 4 (3): 93–97.

Al-Khatib, Nabil. 2002. *Palestinian media and the effects of new Arab media on the information process in Palestine.* Paper presented at the Conference on New Media and Change in the Arab World, Amman, Jordan, 2002. www.media.arabia.org/userfiles/ACF8A8C.doc (accessed 15 August 2003).

Al Rasheed, Anas. 1998. *Professional values. A survey of working journalists in the Kuwaiti daily press.* Unpublished doctoral dissertation, Southern Illinois University.

___ 2001. *Communication and media in the Arab world* (in Arabic), 2nd ed. Beirut: Center for Arab Unity Studies.

Al-Shabbab, Swales J. 1986. Rhetorical features of Arab and British news broadcasts. *Anthropological Linguistics* 28 (1): 31–42.

Alterman, Jon B. 1998. *New media, new politics? From satellite television to the Internet in the Arab world.* Washington: Institute for Near East Policy.

___ 2002. The effects of satellite television on Arab domestic politics. *Transnational Broadcasting Studies* 9.

Amimour, Mouhi' Al Din. 2003. Between victory and defeat. *Al Sharq Al Awsat,* 28 March.

Amin, Hussein. 2001. Mass media in the Arab states between diversification and stagnation: An overview. In Hafez, Kaj (ed.), *Mass media, politics & society in the Middle East.* Cresskill, NJ: Hampton Press.

Anderson, Bendict. 1983. *Imagined communities: Reflections on the origin and spread of nationalism.* New York: Verso.

Ar-Rayis, Saud. 2003. Satellite wars: Scoop at any cost? *Al Wasat,* 6 October: 12–13.

At-Tayara, Bassam K. 2003. The photo in news media: The strongest . . . and the most truthful witness! *Al Wasat,* 6 February: 14–15.

Aucoin, James. 2002. Investigative journalism. In *American journalism: History, principles, practices.* Sloan, W. David, and Lisa Mullikin Parcell (eds.), Jefferson, NC & London: McFarland.

Ayalon, Ami. 1995. *The press in the Middle East: A history.* New York & Oxford: Oxford University Press.

Ayish, Muhammed. 1991. Foreign voices as people's choices: BBC popularity in the Arab world. *Middle Eastern Studies* 27 (3): 374–388.

___ 1995. Potential effects of direct satellite broadcasting on national television systems in the Arab region (in Arabic). *Journal of Humanities and Social Sciences* 11:394–326.

___ 1997. Arab television goes commercial: A case study of the Middle East Broadcasting Center. *Gazette* 59 (6): 473–494.

___ 2001a. American-style journalism and Arab world television: An exploratory study of news selection at six Arab world satellite television channels. *Transnational Broadcasting Studies* 6 (Spring/Summer 2001).

___ 2001b. The changing face of Arab communications: Media survival in the information age. In Hafez, Kai (ed.), *Mass media, politics & society in the Middle East.* Cresskill, NJ: Hampton Press.

___ 2002a. The impact of Arab satellite television on culture and value systems in Arab countries: Perspectives and issues. *Transnational Broadcasting Studies* 9.

___ 2002b. Political communication on Arab world television: Evolving patterns. *Political Communication* 19:137–154.

Badawi, El Said. 1973. *Levels of contemporary Arabic* (in Arabic). Cairo: Dar Al Maarif.

Barnhurst Kevin, and Diana Mutz. 1997. American journalism and the decline in event-centered reporting. *Journal of Communication* 47 (4): 27–53.

Barnhurst Kevin, and John Nerone. 2001. *The form of news: A history.* New York: Guilford Press.

Barnhurst, Kevin. (forthcoming). *The new long journalism,* chapters 1 & 2.

Barranco, Deborah, and Leonard Shyles. 1988. Arab versus Israeli news coverage in the *New York Times. Journalism Quarterly* 65:178–181

Bekhait, As-Said 1998. *The Egyptian press—News values and false conscience* (in Arabic). Cairo: Al Arabi Publishing.

Bell, Allan. 1991. *The language of news media.* Oxford: Blackwell.

Benson, Rodney. 2001. *The mediated public sphere: A model for cross-national research* (Working paper 2001 series, Center for Culture, Organization and Politics). Berkeley: University of California.

Blumler, Jay G., and Gurevitch, Michael. 1995. *The crisis of public communication.* London: Longman.

Booth, Marilyn. 1992. Colloquial Arabic poetry, politics, and the press in modern Egypt. *International Journal of Middle East Studies* 24 (3): 419–440.

Bourdieu, Peirre. 1984. *Distinction: A social critique of the judgement of taste.* Cambridge: Harvard University Press.

___ 1985. *Language and symbolic power.* Cambridge: Polity Press.

___ 1990. *In other words.* Cambridge: Polity Press.

Brinkley, Joel. 2003. U.S. tells Iran to stay out of Iraq, *International Herald tribune,* 24 April.

Cantarino, Vicente. 1974–76. *The syntax of modern Arabic prose* (three volumes). Bloomington: Indiana University Press.

Cappella, Joseph N., and Kathleen Hall Jamieson. 1997. *Spiral of cynicism: The press and the public good.* New York & Oxford: Oxford University Press.

Cassara, Catherine. 2002. Foreign correspondence. In *American journalism: History, principles, practices.* Sloan, W. David, and Lisa Mullikin Parcell (eds.), Jefferson, NC & London: McFarland.

Center for Media and Public Affairs. 1997. *What the people want from the press.* Executive Summary. www.cmpa.com/archive/wdtpwftp.htm (accessed 5 August 2003).

Chaker, Mohamed Naim. 2003. The impact of globalization on cultural industries in United Arab Emirates. *Journal of the American Academy of Business* 3 (2 January): 323.

Claussen, Dane S. 2002. Economics, business, and financial motivations. In *American journalism: History, principles, practices.* Sloan, W. David, and Lisa Mullikin Parcell (eds.) Jefferson, NC & London: McFarland.

Cole, Richard R., and Donald Lewis Shaw. 1974. Powerful verbs and body language. *Journalism Quarterly* 51:62–66.

Cooper, Anne M. 1986. Comparative study of Third World elite newspapers. In Stevenson, Robert L., and Donald Lewis Shaw (eds.), *Foreign news and the new world information order.* Ames: Iowa State University Press.

Cunningham, Brent. 2003. Toward a new ideal: Rethinking objectivity in a world of spin. *Columbia Journalism Review,* July/August.

Dajani, Nabil H. 1989. *The vigilant press: A collection of case studies. An analysis of the press in four Arab countries.* Paris: UNESCO.

___ 1992. *Disoriented media in a fragmented society: The Lebanese experience.* Beirut: American University of Beirut.

Davies, Humphrey. 2003. CNBC Arabiya: The debut. *Transnational Broadcasting Studies* 11. www.tbsjournal.com/CNBC_Debut.html.

Diamond, Mathew. 2002. No laughing matter: Post-September 11 political cartoons in Arab/Muslim newspapers. *Political Communication* 19 (2): 251–272.

Eid, Mushira. 1990. Arabic linguistics: The current scene. In Eid, Mushira (ed.), *Perspectives on Arabic linguistics I: Papers from the first annual symposium on Arabic linguistics.* Amsterdam & Philadelphia: John Benjamins Publishing Co.

Eide, Martin, and Graham Knight. 1999. Service journalism and the problems of everyday life. *European Journal of Communication* 14.

Ekectrantz. 2001. Postmodern times? A comparative study of temporal construction. A paper presented at the 15th Nordic Conference on Media and Communication Research, Reykjavik, Iceland, 11–13 August 2001.

Elbendary, Amina. 2001. TV meets the madding crowd. *Al Ahram Weekly* 538 (June): 14–20.

El-Nawawy, Mohammed, and Adel Iskandar. 2002a. *Al-Jazeera: How the free Arab news network scooped the world and changed the Middle East.* Washington: Westview Press.

El-Nawawy, Mohammed, and Adel Iskandar. 2002b. The minotaur of "contextual objectivity": War coverage and the pursuit of accuracy with appeal. *Transnational Broadcasting Studies* 9. www.tbsjournal.com/Archives/Fall02/Iskandar.html (accessed 27 August 2003).

El Sarayrah, Mohamed. 1986. Foreign news in two Jordanian newspapers, *Journalism Quarterly* 63:363–365.

El-Sherif, Mahmoud. 1980. The Arab attitude to mass media. *Intermedia* 8 (2): 28–29.

Ennaji, Moha. 1995. A syntactico-semantic study of the language of news in Morocco. *International Journal of the Sociology of Language* 112:97–111.

___ 2002. Comment. *International Journal of the Sociology of Language* 157:71–83.

Esam, N. Khalil. 2000. *Grounding in English and Arabic news discourse.* Amsterdam & Philadelphia: John Benjamins Publishing Company.

Essoulami, Said. 2000. The press in the Arab world: 100 years of suppressed freedom. www.cmfmena.org/magazine/features/100_years.htm (accessed 5 June 2003).

Evensen, Bruce J. 2002. Objectivity. In *American journalism: History, principles, practices.* Sloan, W. David, and Lisa Mullikin Parcell (eds.), Jefferson, NC & London: McFarland.

Fakhri, Ahmed. 1998. Reported speech in Arabic journalist discourse. In Elabbas Benmamoun, Mushira Eid and Niloofar Haeri, (eds.), *Perspectives on Arabic linguistics XI.* Amsterdam, Philadelphia: John Benjamins Publishing Company.

Fandy, Mamoun. 2000. Information technology, trust, and social change in the Arab world. *The Middle East Journal* 54 (3): 379–398.

___ 2003. Commentary. *Al Sharq Al Awsat,* 26 June.

Fedler, Fred et al. 1997. *Reporting for the media.* Fort Worth, TX: Harcourt, Brace College Publishers.

Fellman, Jack. 1973a. Sociolinguistic problems in the Middle Eastern Arab world: An overview. *Anthropological Linguistics* 15 (1): 24–32.

___ 1973b. Language and national identity: The case of the Middle East. *Anthropological Linguistics* 15 (5): 244–249.

Fiske, John. 1987. *Television culture:* London: Routledge.

Galtung, Johan, and Marie H. Ruge. 1973. Structuring and selecting news. In Cohen, Stanley and Jock Young (eds.), *The manufacture of news,* 62–72. London: Constable.

Gans, Herbert J. 1999. *Popular culture & high culture: An analysis and evaluation of taste.* New York: Basic Books.

___ 2003. *Democracy and the news.* Oxford: Oxford University Press.

Geard, Kathrine. 2004. Den hemmelige politimand (in Danish). *Journalisten* 10 (9): 14–15.

Geis, Michael. 1987. *The language of politics.* New York, Berlin & Heidelberg: Springer-Verlag.

Ghareeb, Edmund. 2000. New media and the information revolution in the Arab world: An assessment. *The Middle East Journal* 54 (3).

Gledhill, Christine. 2002. Genre and gender: The case of soap opera. In Hall, Stuart (ed.), *Representation: Cultural representations and signifying practices.* London: Sage/The Open University.

Goldie, Janis. 2003. *Embedded journalism and media ethics in the coverage of the 2003 Iraq war: A historical perspective.* www.ucalgary.ca/md/PARHAD/documents/2003-ForumPaper-Goldie.pdf (accessed 10 December 2003).

Golding, Peter, and Philip Elliott. 1979. *Making the news.* London & New York: Longman.

Green, Norma. 2002. Concepts of news. In *American journalism: History, principles, practices.* Sloan, W. David, and Lisa Mullikin Parcell (eds.), Jefferson, NC & London: McFarland.

Guaaybess, Tourya. 2002. A new order of information in the Arab broadcasting system. *Transnational Broadcasting Studies* 9.

Hachten, William. 1999. *The world news prism: Changing media of international communication,* 5th ed. Ames: Iowa State University Press.

Haeri, Niloofar. 1997. The reproduction of symbolic capital: Language, state, and class in Egypt. *Current Anthropology* 38 (5): 795–816.

___ 2003. *Sacred language, Ordinary people: Dilemmas of culture and politics in Egypt.* New York: Palgrave.

___ 2003b. Arabs need to find their tongue, *Guardian,* 14 June. http://www.guardian.co.uk/comment/story/0,3604,977260,00.html (12 January 2004).

Hafez, Kai, ed. 2001. *Mass media, politics & society in the Middle East.* Cresskill, NJ: Hampton Press.

___ 2002. Journalism ethics revisited: A comparison of ethics codes in Europe, North Africa, the Middle East, and Muslim Asia. *Political Communication* 19 (2): 225–250.

Hamada, Basyoni. 1993. *The agenda-setting role of the media in the Arab region* (in Arabic). Beirut: Centre for Arab Unity Studies.

Hammoud, Mahmoud, and Walid Afifi. 1994. Lebanon. In Kamalipour, R. & H. Mowlana (eds.) *Mass media in the Middle East: A comprehensive handbook.* Westport, CT: Greenwood Press.

Harris, Phil, and Harald Malczek. 1979. *Flow of news in the Gulf.* Paris: UNESCO.

Hartley, John. 2001. *Understanding news.* London: Methuen. (First published in 1982.)

Hefny, Zainab. 2003. Commentary. *Al Sharq Al Awsat.* 21 June 2003.

Hjarvard, Stig. 1992. Reconsidering a paradigm: Galtung & Ruge. An empirical, methodological and theoretical examination of "The Structure of Foreign News" and the "Structural Theory of Imperialism." Paper presented to the IAMCR Scientific Conference, Sao Paulo, Brazil, 16–21 August 1992.

___ 1995a. *Internationale TV Nyheder* (in Danish). Copenhagen: Akademisk Forlag.

___ 1995b. *Nyhedsmediernes rolle i det politiske demokrati* (in Danish). Copenhagen: Statsministeriets Medieudvalg.

___, ed. 2001. *News in a globalized society.* Gothenburg: Nordicom.

___ 2002. The study of international news. In Jensen, Klaus Bruhn (ed.) *A handbook of media and communication research: Qualitative and quantitative methodologies.* London & New York: Routledge.

Hodgson, Godfrey. 1999. Det virtuelle rum: Kræft er en bedre historie end krig (in Danish). *Information* 17 (September): 14.

Holes, Clive. 1993. The uses of variation: A study of the political speeches of Gamal Abd al-Nasir. In Eid, Mushira, and Clive Holes (eds.), *Perspectives on Arabic linguistics V: Papers from the fifth annual symposium on Arabic linguistics.* Amsterdam: John Benjamins Publishing Company.

Holes, Clive. 1995. *Modern Arabic: Structures, functions and varieties.* London: Longman

Holm, Hans-Henrik et al. 2000. *Verden på tilbud. Om udenrigsjournalistik og mediernes udlandsdækning* (in Danish). Copenhagen: Center for Journalistik og Efteruddannelse/Ajour.

Howeidy, Amira. 1999. From right to left. *Al Ahram Weekly* 448 (September): 23–29. http://weekly.ahram.org.eg/1999/448/feature.htm (accessed 22 July 2003).

How the Saudi media covered the Iraq war. 2003. *Al Sharq Al Awsat,* 18 April.

Hussein, Riyad Fayez, and Mohamed Raji Zughoul. 1993. Lexical interference in journalistic Arabic in Jordan. *Language Science* 15 (3): 239–254.

International journalists publish the news, and the news publishes the Arab journalists. 2003. *Al Watan,* 10 April.

Jamal, Amal. 2001. State-building and media regime: Censoring the emerging public sphere in Palestine. *Gazette* 63 (2-3): 263–282.

Janardhan, N. 2003. Media-Mideast: Arab media under fire for anti-U.S. war coverage. *Global Information Network* 12 (June): 1.

Jenkins, Henry. 2001. Convergence? I diverge. *Technology Review,* June: 93.

Jensen, Klaus Bruhn. 1986. *Making sense of the news.* Aarhus, Denmark: Aarhus University Press.

___, ed. 1998. *News of the world: World cultures look at television news.* London: Routledge.

___, ed. 2002. *A handbook of media and communication research: Qualitative and quantitative methodologies.* London: Routledge.

Jones, Adam. 2002. From vanguard to vanquished: The tabloid press in Jordan. *Political Communication* 19 (2): 171–188.

Kamalipour, Yahya, ed. 1995. *The U.S. media and the Middle East: Images and perceptions.* Westport, CT: Greenwood Press.

Karam, Jan Jubran. 1992. *Madkhal ila lughat al-i'lam (Introduction to the language of the media)* (in Arabic), 2nd ed. Beirut: Dar Al jiil.

Kazan, Fayad. 1994. Kuwait. In Kamalipour, Yahya R, and Hamid Mowlana (eds.), *Mass media in the Middle East: A comprehensive handbook.* Westport, CT: Greenwood Press.

Keeler, John D., William Brown, and Douglas Tarpley. 2002. Ethics. In *American journalism: History, principles, practices.* Sloan, W. David, and Lisa Mullikin Parcell (eds.), Jefferson, NC & London: McFarland.

Khalil, Elham. 1983. *The Arab satellite and the flow of information.* Amsterdam: University of Amsterdam.

Khalil, Esam. 2000. *Grounding in English and Arabic news discourse.* Amsterdam & Philadelphia: John Benjamins Publishing Co.

Khazen, Jihad. 1999. Censorship and state control of the press in the Arab world. *The Harvard International Journal of Press Politics* 4 (3): 87–92.

Khodour, Adiib. 1997. *The Arab media on the verge of the twenty-first century: The beginning, development and reality* (in Arabic). Damascus & Cairo: The Arab Center for Strategic Studies.

Khouri, Rami. 1991. The Gulf War: An Arab perspective. *Harper's Magazine* April: 17–19.

___ 2001. Arab satellite TV: Promoting democracy or autocracy? *Jordan Times* 9 (May).

___ 2003. U.S., Arab TV: Each tell only half the story. *National Catholic Reporter* 39 (23): 23.

Kilmer, Paulette D. 2002. The press and government. In *American journalism: History, principles, practices.* Sloan, W. David, and Lisa Mullikin Parcell (eds.). Jefferson, NC & London: McFarland.

Kirat, Mohamed. 1987. *The Algerian news people: A study of their backgrounds, professional orientations and working conditions.* Unpublished doctoral dissertation, Indiana University.

Kock, Christian. 2002. *Forstå verden: Politisk journalistik for fremtiden* (in Danish). Frederiksberg, Denmark: Samfundslitteratur.

Koeppel, Barbara. 1989. *The press in the Middle East: Constraint, consensus, censorship.* Washington: Middle East Research & Information Project.

Leinwand, Donna. 2003. Iraqis can't believe everything they read. *USA Today,* 18 September 2003: A13.

Lund, Anker Brink, ed. 2000. *Først med det sidste: en nyhedsuge i Danmark* (in Danish). Copenhagen: Ajour.

Lund, Anker B. et al. 2001. Danskernes syn på medier og demokrati. Institut for Journalistik, University of Southern Denmark. www.journalism.sdu.dk/html/institut/forskning/Danskernes_syn_paa_medier_og_demokrati/afsnit7.pdf (accessed 5 August 2003).

Maalouf, Amin. 1998. *On identity.* Translated from the French by Barbara Bray. London: Harvill Panther.

McFadden, Tom J. 1953. *Daily journalism in the Arab states.* Columbus: Ohio State University Press.

McQuail, Denis. 2002. *McQuail's mass communication theory,* 4th ed. London: Sage Publications.

Mejlby, Mogens. 1999. *Journalistikkens grundtrin. Fra ide til artikel* (in Danish). Aarhus, Denmark: Ajour.

Merrill, John. 1965. How time stereotyped three US presidents. *Journalism Quarterly* 42:563–570.

Meyer, Philip. 1988. Defining and measuring credibility of newspapers: Developing an index. *Journalism Quarterly* 65:567–574 & 588.

Mindich, David T. Z. 1998. *Just the facts: How "objectivity" came to define American journalism.* New York & London: New York University Press.

Moaw'ad, Muhammad. 2000. *Studies in Gulf media* (in Arabic). Kuwait/Cairo/Algiers: Dar Al Kitab Al Hadith.

Morocco promises open media policy. 2002. www.arabicnews.com, July 12.

Nasser, Munir K. 1979. *Press, politics, and power: Egypt's Heikal and Al-Ahram.* Ames: Iowa State University Press.

___ 1983. News values versus ideology: A Third World perspective. In Martine, L. John, and Anju Grover Chaudhary (eds.), *Comparative mass media systems.* New York: Longman.

___ 1990. *Egyptian mass media under Nasser and Sadat.* (Journalism monographs, Dec. 1990, Number 124). Columbia, SC: Association for Education in Journalism and Mass Communication.

Nossek, Hillel, and Khalil Rinnawi. 2003. Censorship and freedom of the press under changing political regimes: Palestinian media from Israeli occupation to the Palestinian authority. *Gazette: The International Journal for Communications Studies* 65 (2): 183–202.

O'Neill, Onora. 2002. *A question of trust.* Cambridge: Cambridge University Press.

Ostgaard, Einar. 1965. Factors influencing the flow of news. *Journal of Peace Research* 2 (1): 39–63.

Qallab, Salah. 2002. Commentary. *Al Sharq Al Awsat,* 27 June 2002.

Parkinson, Dilworth. 1981. VSO to SVO in Modern Standard Arabic: A study in diglossia syntax. In *Syntactic change* (Monograph No. 25), Johns, Brenda, and David Strong (eds.), 159-176. Ann Arbor: University of Michigan Department of Linguistics.

Parkinson, Dilworth. 1993. Knowing Arabic. Testing Egyptians' MSA abilities. In Mushira, Eid, and Clive Holes (eds.), *Perspectives on Arabic linguistics V: Papers from the fifth annual symposium on Arabic linguistics.* Amsterdam & Philadelphia: John Benjamins Publishing Company.

Parkinson, Dilworth, and Zeinab Ibrahim. 1999. Testing lexical differences in regional standard Arabic. In Benmamoun, Elabbas (ed.), *Perspectives on Arabic linguistics XII.* Amsterdam & Philadelphia: John Benjamins Publishing Company.

Patai, Raphael. 1973. *The Arab mind.* New York: Charles Scribner's Sons.

Patterson, Thomas. 1993. *Out of order.* New York: Alfred A. Knoff.

Patterson, Thomas. 1998. Political roles of the journalists. In Graber, Doris, Dennis McQuail, and Pippa Norris (eds.), *The politics of news: The news of politics.* Washington: Congressional Quarterly, Inc.

Pinker, Steven. 1994. *The language instinct. The new science of language and mind.* London: Penguin Books.

Poniwozik, James. 2003. What you see versus what they see. *Time,* 7 April: 68.

Rachty, Gehan. 1978. Foreign news in nine Arab countries. *Communications and Development Review* 2: 23–25.

Ramadan sales. 2002. *Al Sharq Al Awsat,* 7 November.

Reynolds, Gregg. 2003. Alternative TV. *The Christian Century,* 19 April: 8–9.

Rothstein, Robert L. 1995. Democracy in the Third World: Definitional dilemmas. In Garnham, David, and Mark Tessler (eds.), *Democracy, war, and peace in the Middle East.* Bloomington & Indianapolis: Indiana University Press.

Rubin, Barry. 1979. International news and the American media. In Fascell, Dante B. (ed.), *International news: Freedom under attack*. Beverly Hills, CA: Sage & Center for Strategic and International Studies.

Rugh, William. 1987. *The Arab press: News media and political process in the Arab world*, 2nd ed. Syracuse, NY: Syracuse University Press.

___ 2004. *Arab mass media: Newspapers, radio, and television in Arab politics*. Westport, CT: Praeger.

Saad, Reem. 1998. Shame, reputation and Egypt lovers: A controversy over the nation's image. *Visual Anthropology* 10: 401–412.

Safwat Ash-arif criticizes Arab media. 2002. *Al Bayan*, 25 October.

Said, Edward. 1995/1978. *Orientalism: Western conception of the Orient*. London: Penguin.

___ 1997. *Covering Islam: How the media and the experts determine how we see the rest of the world*. New York: Vintage Books.

Sakr, Naomi. 2001. *Satellite realms: Transnational television, globalization & the Middle East*. London: I B Tauris.

Schudson, Michael. 1978. *Discovering the news: A social history of American newspapers*. New York: Basic Books.

___ 1982. The politics of narrative form: The emergence of news conventions in print and television. *Daedalus* 111: 97–113.

___ 1995. *The power of news*. Cambridge & London: Harvard University Press.

___ 2003. *The sociology of news*. New York: W. W. Norton.

Sensenig-Dabbous, Dima. 2000. Media versus society in Lebanon: Schizophrenia in an age of globalization. *Media Development* XLVII (3): 14–17.

Sharkey, Jacqueline E. 2003. The television war. *American Journalism Review* 25 (4): 18.

Shehab, Shaden. 1999. The press in "between." *Al Ahram Weekly*, 427.

Shouby, Eli. 1951. The influence of the Arabic language on the psychology of the Arabs. *Middle East Journal* 5: 284–302.

Soloway, Colin. 2003. Free and reckless: With Saddam out of power, the country's "news" industry has exploded. *Newsweek* (International edition), 11 August: 22.

Songs of grief, enthusiasm, and peace dominate Egyptian radio. 2003. *Al Sharq Al Awsat*, 2 April.

Sreberny-Mohammadi, Annabelle et al., eds. 1985. *Foreign news in the media: International reporting in 29 countries*. Paris: UNESCO.

Sreberny-Mohammadi, Annabelle. 1998. The media and democratization in the Middle East: The strange case of television. *Democratization and the Media* 5 (2): 179–199.

Stanley, Alessandra. 2003. Lessons well learned from the American networks. *New York Times*, July 10, 2003, E8.

Stevenson, Robert L., and Donald Lewis Shaw, eds. 1984. *Foreign news and the new world information order*. Ames: Iowa State University Press.

Suleiman, Yasir. 2003. *The Arabic language and national identity: A study in ideology*. Edinburgh: Edinburgh University Press.

Symposium on the future of the press. 2003. *Al Sharq Al Awsat*, 22 January.

Tash, Adbulkader T. M. 1983. *A profile of professional journalists working in the Saudi Arabian daily press*. Unpublished doctoral dissertation. Southern Illinois University.

Taweela, Waheed. 2002. New media in the Arab world: The social and cultural impact. Paper presented at the Conference on New Media and Change in the Arab World, Amman, Jordan, 2002. www.media.arabia.org/userfiles/ACF8DF0.doc (accessed 15 August 2003).

Tuchman, Gaye. 1972. Objectivity as strategic ritual: An examination of newsmen's notions of objectivity. *American Journal of Sociology* 77 (4): 660–679.

Turkistani, Ahmed S. 1989. *News exchange via Arabsat & news values of Arab TV news people*. Unpublished doctoral dissertation, Indiana University.

UNDP. 2002. *Arab human development report*. New York: United Nations Development Program.

UNESCO. 2002. *World communication and information report 1999–2000*, Chapter 14. Paris: UNESCO.

Urbina, Ian. 2002. Al Jazeera: Hits, misses and ricochets. *Asia Times Online*, 25 December.

Versteegh, Kees. 1997. The development of classical Arabic. In *The Arabic language*. Edinburgh: Edinburgh University Press. www.nitle.org/arabworld/ (accessed 5 December 2003).

Vos, Tim P. 2002. News writing structure and style. In *American journalism: History, principles, practices*. Sloan, W. David, and Lisa Mullikin Parcell (eds.), Jefferson, NC & London: McFarland.

Warchauer, Mark, Ghada R. El Said, and Ayman Zohry. 2002. Language choice online: Globalization and identity in Egypt. *Journal of Computer-Mediated Communication* 7 (4). www.ascusc.org/jcmc/vol7/issue4/warschauer.html (accessed 5 December 2003).

Waugh, Linda. 1995. Reported speech in journalistic discourse: The relation of function and text. *Text* 15 (1): 129–173.

Westerståhl, Jörgen. 1983. Objective news reporting: General premises. *Communication Research* 10 (3): 403–424.

Wheeler, Deborah L. 2001. The Internet and public culture in Kuwait. *Gazette: The International Journal for Communications Studies*, 63 (2-3): 187–201.

Williams, Julie Hedgepeth. 2002. The purposes of journalism. In *American journalism: History, principles, practices*. Sloan, W. David, and Lisa Mullikin Parcell (eds.), Jefferson, NC & London: McFarland.

Williston, Scottie. 2001. Global news and the vanishing American foreign correspondent. *Transnational Broadcasting Studies* 6. www.tbsjournal.com/Archives/Springs01/Williston.html (accessed 10 August 2003).

Willnat, Lars, and David Weaver. 2003. Through their eyes: The work of foreign correspondents in the United States. *Journalism* 4 (4): 403–422.

Wolfsfeld, Gadi, Rami Khouri, and Yoram Peri. 2002. News about the other in Jordan and Israel: Does peace make a difference? *Political Communication* 19 (2): 189–210.

Yaghi, Qasim. 1981. News report and its communicative significance. In *Sub-Editor* (in Arabic). Beirut: Arab Journalists Union.

Yamani, Mai. 2000. *Changed identities: The challenge of the new generation in Saudi Arabia.* London: The Royal Institute of International Affairs.

Zednik, Rick. 2002. Perspectives on war: Inside Al Jazeera. *Columbia Journalism Review* 40 (6): 44–47.

Zelizer, Barbie, David Park, and David Gudelunas. 2002. How bias shapes the news. Challenging the *New York Times'* status as a newspaper of record on the Middle East. *Journalism* 3 (3): 283–307.

Zhao, Yuezhi. 1998. *Media, market, and democracy in China: Between the party line and the bottom line.* Urbana & Chicago: University of Illinois Press.

Index

About the Author

Noha Mellor lectures in Arabic language and media at the Institute of Middle Eastern Studies, University of Copenhagen, combining research there with her work as a professional journalist.